Oral Reading:
Creative and Interpretive

OTHER BOOKS BY THE JOHNSONS:

Drama: Technique and Philosophy
Church Plays and How to Stage Them
Drama for Classroom and Stage
Shakespeare Vignettes
Directing Methods
Best Church Plays
Psalms for the New Millennium
Drama for Junior High

ORAL READING:
Creative and Interpretive

Albert and Bertha Johnson

South Brunswick and New York: A. S. Barnes and Company
London: Thomas Yoseloff Ltd

© 1971 by A. S. Barnes and Co., Inc.
Library of Congress Catalogue Card Number: 72-146759

A. S. Barnes and Co., Inc.
Cranbury, New Jersey 08512

Thomas Yoseloff Ltd
108 New Bond Street
London W1Y OQX, England

ISBN 0-498-07866-3
Printed in the United States of America

Contents

	Introduction	7
1	Reading Aloud for Pleasure, Profit, and Intercourse	13
2	Rudiments of Reading Aloud	31
3	The Elements of Interpretation	64
4	Kinetics, the Visual Aspects of Oral Interpretation	78
5	Triggering the Imagination: The Mind and Heart of the Matter	97
6	Corporate Reading: Choric Drama, Verse Choir, and Readers' Theatre	114
7	Creative Thinking: The Primal Impetus	155
	Appendix	167
	Index	173

Introduction

Communication is the crying priority in the catastrophic "Now" revolution. We can talk through outer space with phenomenal clarity, but bog down woefully in the exchange of thoughts with neighbors, strangers, and enemies. Computers, mass media, and the plethora of knowledge seem to complicate rather than ameliorate our human relations. No wonder there are those who say the medium is the message. Only the medium seems to get through. No wonder there are those impatient demands that the status quo must go.

The dilemma, though old as man, has bright, new, shiny horns. The horns are bright with unparalleled enlightenment. They are new with problems peculiar to our time. Shiny they are because solutions have not yet appeared to dull their luster. Yet this, like all dilemmas throughout the ages past, can be dehorned by people who can communicate. Whether or not it can be dehorned in time depends upon the timing of those who must do the communicating. Who are they? Who are these noncommunicative people who must communicate?

No need to look for them in far-off places. No need

to look beyond the mirror. We are they. We are hooked, we are horned, we are harnessed with involvement whether we like it or not.

We, all of us who are caught in the accelerating whirl toward a new millennium, are party to the escalation. How we communicate will determine whether we lead or follow. What we communicate will fashion the new millennium and shape the meaning of "Now." Not in the seats of government alone, not in the courts and open forums, but rather in the daily intercourse of mind with mind expressed in well-articulated words is an era of understanding made possible.

The need, the hope, the prospect for some understanding are the incentive for the writing of this book. If, from our three decades of teaching, counseling, writing, and directing, we can bring something pertinent and fresh to oral communication, we must express ourselves. If, through these written words, we may augment the power of the spoken word, then what may be done must be done, because the spoken word is still the common and most universal medium of communication. Most of our verbal communication is spoken or read aloud, and the need to do this well has spurred the writing of many texts, so many that the writing of another should have unparalleled justification.

"Unparalleled justification!" Implied in that remark is something short of total modesty. What grounds have we for assuming such justification? The authorship of half a dozen texts? The authorship of more than a dozen plays, popular and frequently produced? Thirty-odd years of experience? Recognition in the academic and professional world? For some these qualifications might be sufficient. For us, the authors, they are not. The justification of this text must be in its content and in the influence of that content. While we cannot evaluate the latter, we can preview the former.

The content deals with the creative as well as the interpretive aspect of oral communication. Creative thinking, particularly relevant to this time in which problem-solving is an urgent part of personal, community, national, and international life, is vital to communication. Regardless of the onslaught of computerization, the future belongs not to the computers but to the creative minds that will hold dominion over all mechanization. Such dominion can be expected from men and women who are trained to think creatively.

The current clash between tradition and contemporary relevance adumbrates the imperative need for creative communication. The clash, like all the altercations of the past, seems new to the newly enlightened, and, as in the past, the closed reactionary minds resist all change. Much-needed avant ventures such as student involvement, ethnic studies, and experimental programs advance apace when issues are approached creatively and viewpoints voiced with clear, dispassionate articulation.

Can this, another textbook on Oral Interpretation, contribute toward such ends? The content must make answer. The content differs from that of most other texts, but merely to differ is not enough. There must be relevance in the difference and, in that relevance, the student should find a practical fairway to excellence. He should, and will, it is hoped, find ways of sharpening his skills and means for expanding his purview and adding dimension to his total concept of life.

Reading for pleasure, profit, and intercourse, as discussed in chapter 1, for instance, may give the student a new perspective on the importance of reading aloud. In chapter 2, Rudiments of Reading Aloud, the basic principles of reading are presented in a way that is somewhat heterodox, while in chapter 3, The Elements of Interpretation, are pinpointed and discussed in terms of practical application.

Chapter 4, entitled "Kinetics, the Visual Aspects of Oral Interpretation," deals with the dynamics of movement, the use of face and body, and the basic gestures, all potential phases of communication often neglected. Imagination, which is the mind and heart of the matter, is the subject of chapter 5, and here we discuss new methods of developing imagination. Chapter 6, "Corporate Reading," covers choric drama, verse choir, and readers' theatre with detailed explanation of techniques for each, as well as some comment on both the therapeutic and artistic aspects of corporate reading. The final chapter deals with creative thinking and offers suggested techniques for developing this power. The chapter also includes examples of creative projects, selected for their possible stimulation potentials. Chapter 7 is followed by a bibliography of carefully chosen pieces for oral reading, many of which are new.

The fact that only chapter 7 has the word "creative" in the title is somewhat misleading. Actually, the creative aspect of communication is as germane to the total content quite as much as is the interpretive aspect. This is inevitable, since the authors believe that oral communication is both interpretive and creative, and that the two aspects should be harmoniously blended in something like a marriage that is made, if not in heaven, then in a heavenly state of knowledge and application.

Oral Reading:
Creative and Interpretive

1

Reading Aloud for Pleasure, Profit, and Intercourse

Every literate person should be able to read aloud. Few can. At least, few can do it effectively. Yet the ability to read aloud is a source of personal power and a hallmark of distinction. It is an ability that opens doors to innumerable opportunities and clears the haze from intellectual horizons. He who can read aloud effectively can affect society and widen his world. He can be a viable instrument of change in this age of rapid change.

Every literate person does read aloud from time to time. He has to. It is a part of business, social, and professional intercourse. Scores of items, in the course of a day, can best be communicated orally, and often must be so communicated. A letter, written instructions, a story in the daily press, a line or two of humor, the minutes of the meeting, a reference in support of a viewpoint, a favorite passage are but a few of the many common articles that may have to be read aloud to an audience of one or many.

Will such reading be a chore and a bore, or will it be pure pleasure? The answer may be found in the pages ahead. That oral reading can be pleasurable is our immediate proposition. We shall discuss the monetary aspects of reading for profit, and shall return again to the subject of intercourse, but let us now explore the opportunities of reading for fun.

To be sure, there is a pleasure aplenty in silent reading, not that it is always pleasurable, nor need it be, yet there is a satisfaction in the covering of content and there is much to be said in favor of silent reading, including speed reading. Indeed, silent reading is more of a necessity than ever if we are to add our fire to the information explosion. However, our concern here is with oral reading. Therefore, henceforth, when we use the word "reading" we will mean oral reading.

Reading is relevant. That is the first thing to keep in mind. Anything that is not relevant in this period of educational revolution simply has no place in the arena of living. Reading is relevant, but relevant to what? The nature of its relevance is the key to diverse pleasures it incites. Let us examine the relevance of reading in terms of both tradition and current trends.

The long-time relevance of reading to liberal arts is obvious. Both in the Western world and in the Orient, reading—and let us remember we are talking about oral reading—has been a trenchant part of liberal education for centuries. Starting in the grade schools students are taught to read aloud, and virtually every college and university in the land has courses in Oral Interpretation. Prior to the fairly recent inclusion of such courses in the academic curriculum, reading was enjoyed in a variety of literary societies prevalent in both England and America. In the judgment of some scholars reading is tantamount to the liberal arts training. Presumably, a person with a liberal education knows how to read and read well. Reading, then, is relevant to liberal arts, but now comes the shocker question. Just how relevant are the liberal arts? The question was a shocker when first asked. Now the questioning is prevalent and relevant in itself.

Just how relevant is it to train young men and women in the liberal arts of learning at a time when involvement in living seems to have priority? The question is a challenge that is being met with several adventuresome innovations, one of which is the approach of the new Johnston College of the University of Redlands. Dr. Pressley McCoy, the first Chancellor of Johnston College, approached higher learning with a threefold program defined as Inter-Personal, Inter-Cultural, and International. The curriculum is geared to those three areas, and there are few classes, no departments, no grades, much independent study, and many seminar discussions. Will graduates of such an institution be members of the learned gentry, or will they be learned men and women fittingly prepared for life in the new millennium? The years will tell and what they tell will be an assessment of relevance.

One thing is certain. The need to read is clearly enhanced. The avant leadership will need to be articulate, and the mastery of articulation is a reward of reading. We speak here of articulation, not merely in the diction connotation, but rather as it relates to the expression and communication of thoughts and ideas. Communication cannot be otherwise than relevant, and its relevance is to all learning, all problem-solving, all efforts to sustain and advance the best of civilization, and all endeavors toward peaceful coexistence with sister nations and all those so-called minority peoples who form the vast majority of mankind. The kind of reading wanted now is reading relevant to crisis, change, and challenge. Can there be fun in any situation so formidable? Does all this set the stage for pleasure reading?

The answer is affirmative, though not at once apparent as such. No mere nostalgic resurrection of the past will serve our ends toward pleasure; not that alone, at least. The affirmation is in the clash with "Now," and yet the Now cannot escape the past. The notion that it can be otherwise is the cardinal error of the Now generation. There is no "Now" except the consequence of cause, and cause is forever entangled in tradition. Sow those seeds of tradition which tradition always bears and so will grow tomorrow's flowers and nightshades: the beautiful and ugly; the good and ill; the progeny of other, former goods and ills.

Our reading pleasure, then, comes not from current camp nor does it come alone from halcyon days of yore. It comes from neither and yet from both. It is in the fusion of the two that we can find meaning for our time. That is the ancient pattern, the pattern that must be rediscovered age after age. In that discovery lies the trail to pleasure, the pleasure of reading. With that discovery we read for meaning, new meaning pertinent to our purpose, and purpose gives incentive to our pleasure.

So then, to read for pleasure is to illumine the present with the light of the past, and, in that light, seek new directions. Read aloud the following psalm (VIII, 3, 4) which the astronauts from Apollo 11 read from outer space and see how applicable it is to the expanding space age. "When I consider thy heavens, the work of thy fingers, the moon and the stars, which thou hast ordained; What is man, that thou art mindful of him?"

Now read aloud the following excerpts from some of

the plays of ancient Greece and apply them to a current problem.

> I care for riches, to make gifts
> To friends, or lead a sick man back to health
> With ease and plenty. Else small aid is wealth
> For daily gladness; once a man be done
> With hunger, rich and poor are all as one.
> Euripides, *Electra*

> I think that Fortune watcheth o'er our lives,
> Surer than we. But well said: he who strives
> Will find his gods strive for him equally.
> *Ibid.*

> There lives no greater fiend than Anarchy;
> She ruins states, turns houses out of doors,
> Breaks up in rout the embattled soldiery.
> Sophocles, *Antigone*

> Men of perverse opinion do not know
> The excellence of what is in their hands
> Till some one dash it from them.
> Sophocles, *Ajax*

> "Towers and ships are nothingness,
> Void of our fellow men to inhabit them."
> Sophocles, *Oedipus Tyrannus*

> So in the Libyan fable it is told
> That once an eagle, stricken with a dart,
> Said, when he saw the fashion of the shaft,
> "With our own feathers, not by others' hands,
> Are we now smitten."
> Fragment by Aeschylus

Careful and intensive listening to what we read and to how we read it will do two things in addition to sharpening our awareness of the parallel between the past and now. It will heighten our appreciation of the thing we are reading and, indubitably, shock us into a realization that we need some help in reading. The help will come later in this text and, with that help, the appreciation will increase even more.

Meanwhile, read on and on for pleasure. Read for the pleasure of discovering new facts and fictions, and rediscovering old favorites. Read for the excitement of finding new meanings and for the fun of trying to articulate those meanings. Read for remembrance of things past and the fitting of those things into the present. Read for the pleasure of listening to yourself and for the pleasure you may give to other listeners. Read for the sheer fun of reading.

Implicit in the above consideration of relevance is the idealistic suggestion that relevance relates only, or at least primarily, to the general improvement of human relations, expecially in the areas of politics, social equality, and a better state of affairs for everyone who has been getting the short end of things. There is another side of the relevance coin. It is the "heads I win" side. It is the commercial side. It is the side that shows the personal pecuniary potentials. What about that kind of relevance? What does a marked ability to read aloud have to do with that? How does reading improve the individual's chances toward getting ahead financially?

It is reasonable to suspect that this commercial relevance is the very crux of the whole liberal arts controversy. Historically, study of the liberal arts is a gentleman's luxury. Now, with more than six million young people in college, it may be a luxury that is somewhat passé. One is prone to surmise that there aren't that many gentlemen left in our shifting society, at least not that many gentlemen in the nineteenth-century sense of the word. Ergo many, if not most, of those six million are in college to improve their monetary prospect quite as much as to enrich their learning. This being the case, the complexion of the liberal arts has altered or, where it hasn't altered, it is in line for alterations. Of course there is an alternative in the fact that more students can be channeled into technical and vocational schools. However, even in such schools oral reading can contribute enormously to the student's advancement. Technicians, engineers, computer programmers, and even plumbers need to be articulate in their oral communication.

If we seem guilty of some circumlocution, it is only to accent the point made above. What is the relevance of reading to personal take-home pay? The same question could be asked of many other academic subjects. The answer is, "background." However, in the case of reading, something in addition to background is included. It is skill. Skill in reading a page of print, or a page of copy, and communicating the content to another person or group of persons is a valuable asset for any citizen of our republic. Two technicians, for example, may be equal in all other qualifications, but if one of them can read and communicate directions better than the other, he will be the one to advance more rapidly.

So much by way of answering the question, "What shall it profit a man if he knows how to read?" However, there is another aspect to this subject of reading for profit. Thus far we have limited our discussion to those individuals who realize an increment from their training in reading indirectly. Now let us give some thought to all those people whose careers are more or less dependent on their ability to read. Who are they? Their number is larger than many people may imagine. We are not referring merely to the handful of professionals who play the lecture circuits presenting public readings, though certainly they must be included. Again, there are more of them than many may suppose. Here for example, is a partial list of professionals and semi-professionals who spend a part or all of their time engaging in such entertainment: Lowell Thomas, Dick Gregory, J. Edgar Hoover, Richard Nixon, Hal Holbrook, Hugh Downs, Ralph J. Bunche, Ralph Nader, Art Buchwald, Drew Pearson, Al Capp, Arthur Goldberg, Victor Borge, Glenn T. Seaborg, John Raitt, Mort Sahl, Justice William Douglas, Norman Vincent Peale, R. H. Edwin Espy, Ralph Abernathy, Edwin Aldrin, Michael Collins, Neil Armstrong, John Glenn, Walter Schirra, S. Hayakawa, Edward Kennedy, and Hubert Humphrey.

We could add to this list several thousand professors, politicians, ministers, actors, teachers, doctors, businessmen, and the like who make diverse public appearances annually, usually for a substantial honorarium, nearly all of whom do some reading in the course of their programs. However, the list of people whose careers are related directly to their reading skill does not stop with these. Far from it. These are but a bevy in the throng. Let us quickly survey those reading-oriented professions.

There is, most obviously, the law profession. Students intent on a career in law greatly improve their chances of being accepted in law schools when they have had training in oral interpretation and acting. We who write this book can make that statement with empirical authority because we have had many students accepted for law graduate schools largely on the strength of their courses with us.

Why is this the case? The answer is obvious. Lawyers

must know how to read and read aloud. Rare is the case that is argued without some reference to material that must be read to the court, and the lawyer who cannot do this effectively is not likely to suffer from a plethora of cases. Cases are won and cases are lost by attorneys who read well or read poorly. Juries and judges are susceptible to reading that is clear, articulate, and communicative. Most of us are so unfamiliar with the jargon of jurisprudence that we must have the language read with intelligent interpretation.

Ministers must read. Even those rare ones who memorize their sermons or speak extemporaneously still read the scriptural text, and that, as every good churchgoer knows, can be either boringly painful or pleasantly exciting. The reading of scripture can be an art in itself. Some seminaries give this matter rigorous recognition. If more did, church attendance might increase. Pity the poor pastor who stumbles through the scripture lesson or proclaims it in a ministerial wail. As is the case with law, oral interpretation is an excellent prerequisite to training in homiletics.

Actors don't count. Their words are memorized. Yet in a sense they do count among the people whose careers depend on reading, because the lines they speak were read many times before they were committed to memory. Furthermore, they had to read in auditions in order to get cast. Actors, more than most professionals, must be expert in interpretation. Our conviction in this matter is so strong that we urge all our acting students to take work in oral communication. This is the case in many universities. In most departments of Theatre Arts there is ample opportunity for students to study oral interpretation.

In radio and television careers are rigorously related to reading ability. Announcers, commentators, and actors all read, if not from scripts, from teleprompters. In the case of announcers and commentators, much of what they read is often sight reading, which takes a special skill, a skill based on the fundamentals of oral reading. Unique in this medium is the commercial. If ever oral communication is called for anywhere it is in the radio and television commercials. In this operation the voice must "sell." That calls for extra expertise. Yet it is an expertise included in the oral-reading training. Of course, it must be admitted that all commercials do not sell, and all announcers do not communicate. Any brief bit of channel-hopping will usually result in a fine collection of flubs, sinful syntax, incredible diction, and voices that are inimitably bad. The medium could use a corps of good speech teachers.

Speaking of teachers, let us speak further of them—and not of speech teachers only but of all who serve in the vast teaching profession. It would be safe to surmise that rare is the day on which a teacher, any teacher from pre-school to graduate school, is not called upon to read something aloud. Reading is a commodity that comes with the teaching territory. He may lecture, he may ad lib, he may discuss informally, but somewhere along the way he will have to read, and read distinctly, if he wants to hold his class. "He," of course, is generic, and should read "she" as well. He the teacher or she the teacher is a reader, and what a wondrous world would waken if he or she would always read with meaning, zest, and challenge. To that end we hope. To that end we try to train. To that end this book is dedicated. When we have teachers who can communicate the greatest of man's recorded words, we will have greatness in our culture.

The men and women who legislate for us at city, county, state, and federal level are readers, all. They cannot legislate without the talent to communicate. What they communicate, more often than not, comes from the printed page and must be interpreted intelligently to others. They, and virtually everyone who serves in government and politics as well as those aspiring to political careers, are helped or hindered by their capacity to read. When they read well, they may do well in their careers. When they read poorly, their careers are likely to be short-lived. To the politicians we must add those tens of thousands who serve our country in foreign diplomacy and the many branches of domestic government, and those who command our military forces and those who serve the military, and likewise, those who are in articulate opposition and speak the democratic voice of honest dissent.

Whoever speaks affirmatively or in dissent will win more ears with eloquence than with force, and find the thrust of well-written words well read far more effective in the long run than petulant, impassioned shouts of mindless slogans. Strong, rational, articulate reading of vibrant, moving ideas, historic and spontaneous, is the means of progress. It is the leaders who read and speak persuasively who ultimately make history. They are the positive builders who carry on in the wake of all that the nihilists negate.

This leads us to the intercourse of oral reading. We are engaged in intercourse in all our current conflicts. Intercourse is at the crux of conflict. Conflict is the impetus to progress. Through reasonable and compassionate intercourse we can progress at both the universal and the personal levels. We read of controversies of the past and from that past gain knowledge and encouragement to cope with problems of our time, problems that involve us personally, regionally, nationally, and internationally. We read, and through our reading communicate the wisdom of the ancients to our peers in quest of wisdom. We read the wise men of our time and try their wise words on for size, and, when they seem to fit, we pass them on to friends and colleagues through the intercourse of reading and whatever argument the reading prompts.

The daily intercourse in which we all engage both fashions and reflects our personal relations, and dominion over personal relations is one of the highest goals of education. All that we think and do, and read, and say, and all that we are, influences our daily intercourse with those whose lives we touch. All that we think and do and say and are is affected by what we read, and what we read aloud affects whoever hears it. Thanks to our heritage we can enhance, enliven, and enrich our intercourse with such personal-relations guides as the following excerpts:

> The very spring and root of honesty and virtue lie in the felicity of lighting on good education.
> Plutarch, *Of the Training of Children*

> It is indeed a desirable thing to be well descended, but the glory belongs to our ancestors.
> *Ibid.*

> It is a point of wisdom to be silent when occasion requires, and better than to speak, though never so well.
> *Ibid.*

> The whole life of man is but a point of time; let us enjoy it, therefore, while it lasts, and not spend it to no purpose.
> *Ibid.*

> Like the man who threw a stone at a bitch, but hit his stepmother, on which he exclaimed, "Not so bad!"
> Plutarch, *On the Tranquillity of the Mind*

Either death is a state of nothingness and utter unconsciousness, or, as men say, there is a change and migration of the soul from this world to another.

Socrates, *Apology*

No evil can happen to a good man, either in life or after death.
Ibid.

Take heed that ye do not your alms before men, to be seen of them.

Matthew V, 13

They think that they shall be heard for their much speaking.

Matthew V, 7

Take therefore no thought for the morrow; for the morrow shall take thought for the things of itself. Sufficient unto the day is the evil thereof.

Matthew VI, 34

Or what man is there of you, whom if his son ask bread, will he give him a stone?

Matthew VII, 8

Therefore all things whatsoever ye would that men should do to you, do ye even so to them: for this is the law and the prophets.

Matthew VII, 12

False words are not only evil in themselves, but they infect the soul with evil.

Socrates, *Dialogues of Plato, Phaedo*

The soul takes nothing with her to the other world but her education and culture.

Ibid.

Rais'd and swell'd with honours great
   (such on bard yet never sate)
With meekness and modesty he bore him;
And while his laurels grew, he kept ever in his view
   The heights yet unconquer'd before him.

                         Aristophanes, *The Wasps*

He who is of a calm and happy nature will hardly feel the pressure of age.

                         Plato, *The Republic,* Book I

When there is an income-tax, the just man will pay more and the unjust less on the same amount of income.

                         Ibid.

Beauty of style and harmony and grace and good rhythm depends on simplicity.

                         Ibid., Book III

Musical training is a more potent instrument than any other, because rhythm and harmony find their way into the inward places of the soul.

                         Ibid.

The judge should not be young; he should have learned to know evil, not from his own soul, but from late and long observation of the nature of evil in others.

                         Ibid.

Wealth is the parent of luxury and indolence, and poverty of meanness and viciousness, and both of discontent.

                         Ibid.

The direction in which education starts a man will determine his future life.

                         Ibid., Book IV

God loveth not the speaking ill of any one in public.
The Koran, chapter 4

If God should punish men according to what they deserve, he would not leave on the back of the earth so much as a beast.
Ibid., chapter 35

Woe be unto those who pray, and who are negligent at their prayer: who play the hypocrites, and deny necessaries to the needy.
Ibid., chapter 107

If there be righteousness in the heart, there will be beauty in the character. If there be beauty in the character, there will be harmony in the home. If there be harmony in the home there will be order in the nation. If there be order in the nation, there will be peace in the world.
Confucius

What you do not want done to yourself, do not do to others.
Ibid.

Pride should not be allowed to grow. The desire should not be indulged. The will should not be gratified to the full. Pleasure should not be carried to excess.
Ibid.

By poetry, the mind is aroused. By music, the finish is received. The odes stimulate the mind. They include self-contemplation. They teach the art of sensibility. They help to regulate resentment. They bring home the duty of serving one's father and one's prince.
Ibid.

Those who know, don't say, and those who say, don't know.
Lao-tse

Bide in silence and the radiance of the spirit shall come in and make its home.
Ibid.

The way to do is to be.
Ibid.

One who would guide a leader of men in the uses of life will warn him against the use of arms for conquest.
Ibid.

The way for a vital man to go is not the way of a soldier. Only the man who recognizes all men as members of his own body is a sound man to guard them.
Ibid.

Heaven arms with compassion those whom she would not see destroyed.
Ibid.

There is a being, wonderful, perfect, that existed before heaven and earth. How quiet it is! How spiritual it is! It stands alone, and it does not change. It moves around and around, but does not, on this account, suffer. All life comes from it. It wraps everything with its love as in a garment. Yet it claims no honor. It does not demand to be lord. I do not know its name, and so I call it Tao, The Way, and I rejoice in its power.
Ibid.

If there were no God, it would be necessary to invent him.
Voltaire

If This is best of possible worlds, what then are the others?
Ibid.

Optimism is the madness of maintaining that everything is right when it is wrong.
Ibid.

This is the happiest of mortals, for he is above everything he possesses.
Ibid.

Let us work without disputing; it is the only way to render life tolerable.
Ibid.

I hold every man a debtor to his profession.
Francis Bacon

No pleasure is comparable to the standing upon the vantage-ground of truth.
Ibid.

Revenge is a kind of wild justice, which the more man's nature runs to, the more ought law to weed it out.
Ibid.

Prosperity is the blessing of the Old Testament; adversity is the blessing of the New.
Ibid.

Virtue is like precious odours,—most fragrant when they are incensed or crushed.
Ibid.

As these quotations and the preceding passages suggest, reading aloud is for pleasure, for profit, and for intercourse. However, reading aloud is not so simple as it sounds, and certainly not so easy as this chapter may have implied. Some, the uninitiated, may think that anybody can pick up a book and start reading aloud. Anyone, or almost anyone, could, but would the author's meaning be conveyed? Would what is being read be interesting to the listener? Would the voice of the reader sound vibrant and pleasant, or flabby and dull? Would the reader be able to sustain, to project, to enunciate, to read with expression, with variety, with feeling, with intelligence, with relaxation, with concentration, with clear, clean communication, and with rapport with the listener? These are but a few of the questions we shall now consider, questions which should make the ensuing chapters the meaty part of the book.

2

Rudiments of Reading Aloud

One of the best ways to discover the rudiments of reading is to listen to someone read aloud. If he reads well he may be worth emulating. If he reads badly, which is more likely to be the case, listening to him may be pure torture, but his poor performance may have much to teach you. Listening is itself an art. In fact, it is the first art to be mastered as we seek the discovery of rudiments. Listening calls for concentration. Concentration means being alert, aware, sensitive, and responsive.

In order to become a good listener, we must first school ourselves in concentration. Most students of acting are familiar with various exercises in concentration. Any or all such exercises can be applied with gratifying results to the art of reading. It should be helpful at this point to review what Richard Boleslavsky has to say about concentration.

Richard Boleslavsky, a product of the Moscow Arts

Theatre, has for years been a mentor to many an actor, but his excellent advice is certainly not limited to actors only. What he has to say about concentration, for example, is useful to every one who is concerned with developing self-discipline.

In one of his celebrated lessons, Boleslavsky asks a young woman student if she has ever observed some one absorbed completely in what he was doing—a ship's pilot, for instance, or a scientist, an architect, or possibly an actor waiting in the wings for his entrance. The student replies that she once observed a great star in the wings, but that the star was not aware of her. To which Boleslavsky adds that the actor was probably not aware of anybody else or any other thing around him. He was thinking only about his role and his entrance. Then he explains that concentration is the quality which permits one to channel all his emotional and intellectual powers toward one definite goal or object.

Any person who has mastered the ability to concentrate can hold his focus on a particular project as long as it pleases him to do so, and often even beyond the point of pleasure. Boleslavsky tells the story of a fisherman who spent forty-eight hours at the rudder of his craft during a storm. His concentration carried him beyond the point of normal physical endurance, and only when his craft was safely in port did he allow his body to collapse and give way to fatigue. Such strength, such control, such certainty of power over self is a fundamental quality of every creative artist. Each creative person must find it within himself and develop it to the ultimate degree.

But how? The student naturally wants to know. She is admonished not to hurry. Patience is an aspect of concentration. The pilot has his compass, the scientist his microscope, the architect his drawings, but these are all external objects of concentration. There are also internal objects of concentration. For example, what is it that the actor concentrates on?

His role? Of course, but there is something more. All through rehearsals there is concentration of a kind, but it is a searching type of creativity. Only when the role is mastered does the actor begin to concentrate constructively. Only then is he free to truly focus on the creative aspect of his acting.

Boleslavsky then asks the student to define what acting is. Somewhat taken aback, she says that acting is to act, just to act, and, fumbling for words that don't come, adds that she really doesn't know, at which Boleslavsky chides her for wanting to devote her life to something she actually doesn't know the meaning of.

Then the master explains that acting is the life of the soul experiencing birth through art. So, for the actor, the object of concentration is the human soul. Throughout the period of preparation, the object of concentration for the actor is his soul and the souls of the other players with whom he works. In performance, however, the object is his own soul. This means that, in order to act, one must be able to concentrate on something imperceptible, or something perceptible only by penetrating the depths of one's own identity. Through such concentration, one may recognize what would be evidenced in life only in a moment of intense emotion. What is called for is a concentration on emotions which do not actually exist but must be conjured up through imagination.

At this point the student seems lost, because she wants to know how in the world one can develop in one's self something that does not exist. To this Boleslavsky replies that one does not start with a Chopin nocturne, but with five finger exercises, and then goes on to explain that the five finger exercises for the actor are the five senses. Just as the fingers are able to ultimately play scales and arpeggios, so the senses can become highly sensitized. Touch, taste, smell, sight, and hearing can all be made more sensitive through exercises in concentration. The senses are the key to enriched creation, and are as essential to such creation as are the mastery of scales to the playing of a Chopin nocturne. As a musician learns to master musical scales, so an actor develops the mastery of concentration with the five senses. It is possible to learn to create with one's entire being by concentrating on the various senses—by deliberately going about the task artificially. This is done by giving the five senses diverse problems, and concentrating on creative solutions.

Here the student protests that she does know how to feel and how to listen. In life, perhaps, agrees Boleslavsky, but probably not on stage. No, on stage, too, the student protests. The master challenges this by asking her to listen to an imaginary mouse scratching in the corner.

The first thing the student wants to know is where the audience is. That is of no consequence, the master assures her, and is appalled at the girl's fake gestures of listening. He is equally appalled at her artificial response to an imaginary orchestra he asked her to listen to.

By this process, Boleslavsky has tricked the young actress into revealing her inability to listen honestly. She can only pretend to listen, and her pretense is purely theatrical. She must learn to concentrate spiritually. She can neither create emotions, nor is she in possession of her own senses, the master points out.

How can she ever learn? She can learn by hard daily exercises which the master says he can give her by the thousands, adding that she can probably add another thousand if she cares to think about it.

Then will she be an actress? No, there is more to it than that. To listen, to feel, to look, to touch, to smell, to do all these things and do them honestly is essential but only elementary. She must learn to do all those things in a hundred different ways, as a hundred different characters.

Boleslavsky gives us some idea of what power there can be in the mastery of concentration. He does this by asking the student to pretend she is on stage at the opening of the first act. She is listening to a departing motor car. Her listening must be so convincing that it arrests the attention of a restless audience. One person may be thinking about his stock exchange gains or losses, another about the dinner he has just had, another about a business problem, and another about a pretty girl a few seats away. The attention of all those individuals, along with hundreds more in the audience, must be immediately gained and sustained to the extent that they forget their own problems and interests and give their full focus to that girl on stage who is listening to a departing automobile. What she is doing takes command of their minds. She, the actress, must become the most important person in the world for them. There, in that moment in that place, she becomes the center of the spectator's world. That is the kind of concentration a performer has to have, and it is a humbling though exalting power. To make others feel that they have no right to intrude on your concentration, that what they have been thinking about is inconsequential to your moment in the sun is an ability to be envied, but entirely achievable.

How does one achieve such power? Boleslavsky gives some specifics. He is talking about acting, but his advice is applicable to any one concerned about improving his powers of concentration. It is all a matter of talent and technique. There must of course be talent. Without talent all the technique that can be learned is of little use, but talent alone is not enough. Technique involves the training of body, mind, and soul.

The education of the body leads to control and coordination. Every muscle and every nerve must be trained to respond promptly to the will. This, as Boleslavsky points out, involves gymnastics, fencing, dance, games calling for physical skills, and a variety of body exercises. In addition there are breathing exercises, vocalizing drills, and drills in diction and voice projection.

It is interesting to have Boleslavsky say these things for us at this time, because most of what he says is in line with a recurring theme throughout this book. Certainly most of what he says will be recapitulated, and with added dimension. His suggestions to the young student regarding the training of the mind are prologue to things to be dealt with later.

In the training of the mind, background becomes an all-important element. One can discuss Shakespeare, Molière, and other great persons in drama only with people who know something about those giants. This would be true in any field, of course. The more cultural background one has, the more potentials there are for one's mind to probe. Some knowledge of history, literature, art, and science, some breadth and depth of cultural purview, and some sensitivity to humanity and the humanities are essential as indispensable aspects of intellectual training. In short, the more background one has to fall back on, the more one's ability to concentrate will be enhanced.

Boleslavsky believes that the memory must be developed, particularly the memory of feelings along with the memory of inspiration, imagination, and penetration.

Along with this, the visual memory must be greatly developed. In addition, he urges the expansion of faith in imagination and in faith itself. Other faculties to be developed are observation, the will, a capacity to express diverse emotions, and, as we might expect, he adds the development of a sense of humor as well as a tragic sense.

We have felt it worth while to discuss the Boleslavsky theory of concentration, not only because it seems sound and practical and is extremely helpful to students, but because of his high histrionic ideals. He believes that the power to create and the power to interpret are two of the highest gifts to mankind. With those gifts, or should we say achievements, one should be able to contemplate life's two greatest mysteries, the mystery of perfection, and the mystery of the eternal.

When we listen with concentration we can begin to analyze the reading we are hearing. Immediately we will become aware of what is good and what is bad, and gradually we can distinguish the causes that make it good or bad. First comes a general, overall impression. Then, as we listen carefully we become aware of details such as voice quality, diction, phrasing, and variety or lack of it. Let us assume that the reading to which we are listening is very bad. If it is being badly done, what is it that is bad about it? Let us examine the things that are most likely to be bad about it.

We may begin with the voice itself. It may be too throaty, or too nasal, or too palatal, or it may be too loud or too soft, or it may be lacking in resonance. It may be thin, or gravelly, or too plosive, or it may be totally lacking in musical tone.

With this analysis, we have arrived at rudiment number one, *voice control*. We have arrived at rudiment number one, but we are not yet ready to discuss it. First we must consider those two elements that are basic to voice control, relaxation and breathing.

In order to read with any degree of mastery over the voice, it is necessary to be free of tension. Most of the bad elements mentioned above can be traced to tension. Sadly enough, people can be tense without knowing it. Tension anywhere in the body can cause tension in the voice and often cause other areas of the body to tighten up to the detriment of stance, stability, and stamina.

Recently a girl with a voice problem was amazed to discover that her problem came basically from her posture. She was allowing her shoulders to hump, which in turn caused her to stick her chin out and forced her arms and hands to turn in like those of an ape. This unnatural posture was creating tension, and that tension was blocking the free flow of air through her larynx and causing her to speak with a tight, squeaky voice. A few trips up and down stairs with a heavy book on her head with her tummy and her chin pulled into position soon worked the desired miracle for her.

A young man who used to get laryngitis almost every time he had a performance in immediate prospect discovered that his laryngitis was nothing but a case of stage-fright tension. Faithful adherence to a set of daily relaxation drills shortly relieved his laryngitis attacks. Such drills are readily available in any number of books about oral interpretation as well as in acting texts, but nobody ever benefited much from merely reading those drills. Drills are for doing, and we offer a few at this point that are well calculated to foster relaxation.

1. Lie flat on your back, preferably on the floor or a hard surface. In that position tense all your muscles, making your entire body as stiff as possible. Then let go like a pricked balloon. Let every portion of your body go

utterly limp. After three or four rounds of this, try tensing slowly, beginning with the feet and working gradually up the legs, through the torso, into the arms and shoulders, and finally the neck and face. Hold for several counts in complete tension, then gradually relax the face, then the neck, then shoulders and arms, and so on down through the feet. Repeat from three to six times.

2. Yawn. Yawn and stretch. Standing in a comfortable position, lift your arms up and slightly back, raise your chin, and open your mouth and gently ease yourself into a relaxing yawn. Indulge in a series of good yawns. This is one of the best ways to relax the throat muscles, a prime requisite for voice control.

3. Still standing in a comfortable position, swing your body from side to side, letting your arms swing freely. This drill is enhanced by picking a focal point some distance away and pretending that you are brushing that point with your nose. This has the added effect of resting the eyes.

4. Standing by a chair, preferably a soft one, sink slowly and with control into a sitting position. Rise, stiffen, tensing all the muscles in your body, then let go and fall into the chair with utter relaxation. After sitting a moment, rise, using only the muscles essential to get you to your feet, and walk a few steps, giving in to the pull of gravity. Return to the chair, taking care to make a marked difference between the moments of tension and those of relaxation. The idea is to discipline your body to go from extreme tension to complete relaxation on command.

5. Sit cross-legged, Buddha fashion, on the floor, with hands folded across your stomach and eyes half closed. Should this excursion into Zen prove too uncomfortable, settle for a cozy sitting position on a chair with hands folded and eyes half closed. Sit there for at least five

minutes, thinking of nothing in particular. To think of nothing is difficult, in fact next to impossible, for most of us, at least at first, but do the best you can. Breathing softly the word "peace" from time to time will help. Here the object is to discipline both the mind and the body in controlled relaxation. This is the ultimate relaxation drill. To master it for a period of even a few minutes will be an achievement, and it will contribute immeasurably to your general relaxation.

Continuing, now, in the interest of voice control, let us take up the matter of breathing. Although people go about breathing all of their lives, it is surprising to discover how few breathe properly. Along with tension, the lack of breath support is the cause of weak and faulty voices. Without breath support it is virtually impossible to maintain any sort of dominion over the voice. Without breath support the voice may crack, or take on a whiney or nasal quality, or be too faint to carry, or force the reader into a choppy, irregular rhythm, causing him to phrase improperly and do declensions on commas instead of reserving them for periods.

Harry, we'll call him Harry, could not get through a sentence of a dozen words without breaking for breath. Mary, we'll call her Mary, could not be heard in the first row. Harry and Mary did some panting exercises. Then they lay on their backs with a weight on their solar plexuses and laughed. As they laughed they bounced the weight up and down. So Harry and Mary learned to breathe. They learned to limber up and strengthen their intercostal muscles, to toughen up their diaphragms, to inhale deep gulps of air and let their voices ride on the exhalation of that air. In short, they learned to breathe. The moral of this true story is obvious. Harry read long sentences with no interruption, and Mary was heard in the back row.

It is a great mistake to assume that students can breathe with control. All too often teachers make this mistake. This is no doubt because improper breathing is not always readily detected. It is immediately apparent in such cases as were mentioned above, but sometimes young readers, like young actors, have enough native vitality to fool us into thinking they are breathing properly when they are only breathing adequately. The trouble with adequate breathing is that it is adequate only up to a point, and anyone who does much with oral reading will soon find himself beyond that point.

Basically, there are three kinds of breathing: high chest, or shallow (all wrong, of course), abdominal (not bad and still used by singers to some extent), and diaphragmatic intercostal (decidedly the best for the spoken word). The person with no training in breathing more often than not breathes high in his chest and controls his exhalation with his throat muscles which, of course, gives him no control over his breath and therefore no control over his voice. High chest breathing can be easily detected by movement of both the chest and the shoulders.

The opposite extreme from high chest breathing is abdominal breathing. This is a legitimate system of controlled breathing, and, in the opinion of some, especially voice instructors, is on a par with or better than diaphragmatic intercostal. In abdominal breathing, the abdomen is projected with inhalation and is pulled back into position with exhalation. In this system, as in diaphragmatic intercostal, the diaphragm, which is the big muscle that encircles the torso at the base of the ribs, is the controlling muscle, with abdominal muscles giving some support.

The diaphragmatic intercostal system takes advantage of the flexibility of the rib cage and allows for a somewhat greater capacity of intake of air. Through exercises, the rib cage is expanded in its capacity and the lungs are allowed to inflate freely. In this system the diaphragm serves as the major control, but it is assisted by the intercostal muscles, which are the muscles that control the rib cage. The advantage of this system over the abdominal system is that it permits the abdomen to be held up in its proper place instead of allowing it to sag and bulge with each inhalation, thus the diaphragmatic intercostal system permits a better posture, which is a strong factor with readers and actors.

There is still another system of breathing which is sometimes taught to advanced students, but it should not be tampered with until one or the other of the above systems is mastered. It is a combination of abdominal and diaphragmatic intercostal and is the breathing used in yoga. The importance of any system is commensurate with the needs and nature of the individual. Each student should experiment until he finds the system best suited to his anatomy and psychology. What is imperative about breathing is that the lungs and controlling muscles be given daily exercises that will develop both and will facilitate control. Deep inhalation done quickly, and slow, even exhalation are the mechanisms to be mastered.

As is the case with relaxation drills, breathing exercises are to be found in many other books, so here we offer but a few of the basic ones.

1. Laugh. Toss your head back and throw your hands up and let go with a lusty, hearty, good, loud laugh. Laughing with several other persons is especially effective, providing you laugh and do not merely giggle. Take an extra deep breath and continue laughing until you have exhausted that breath. Repeat five or six times.

2. If the above exercise is done properly, the diaphragm and intercostal muscles will be working naturally.

With your hand placed at the base of your rib cage, note exactly what happens when you laugh. Now try making those same muscular movements without the laugh. Practice that movement, minus the laugh, several times.

3. Next, pant. With your hands still on the rib cage, continue panting, making certain that there is decided movement at the base of the ribs—ribs out for inhalation, ribs in for exhalation. Continue panting for from twenty to thirty seconds, working gradually up to at least a minute.

4. Standing erect, force all the air out of your lungs. When you think you have emptied your lungs completely, press your lips into a whistling position and continue to breathe out. You will usually discover you have a little breath left. Now, slowly inhale, taking in all the air you can possibly hold, and when you think you have reached your capacity try taking in a little more. Hold your breath for three or four counts, then slowly exhale until you have again completely emptied your lungs. Repeat this drill a half dozen times. This is an excellent exercise for expanding your breathing capacity.

5. While jogging in place, inhale on a count of four, hold your breath for a count of four, then exhale on a count of four. Rest four counts and repeat several times. This drill can be applied to walking as well as jogging. It is particularly good for developing rhythmic breathing.

Voice control, dependent as it is upon relaxation and breath support, is contingent upon voice production. Voice on breath is the essence of voice production. Readers, like speakers and actors, must learn to speak on the breath. This means using the breath rather than wasting it. This means starting the breath slightly, although ever so slightly, ahead of the voice. People without training in breath support often utter an initial sound before releasing the breath. This results in weak, inarticulate attacks, and is an undisciplined use of breath. The flow of the exhalation should be timed with the utterance of the phrase or sentence, and the timing should be such that the breath is not exhausted before the end of the cadence. In fact, there should be breath in reserve, when it is time to take the next inhalation.

In sum, voice control, the first rudiment of reading aloud, is related to and dependent upon relaxation and breath support as well as the actual production of vocal sound.

The production of vocal sound leads to the next rudiment, which is *voice placement*. It could be argued that placement is a part of voice control, but because of our feeling for the importance of voice placement and our special experience in that area we prefer to treat it as a separate rudiment. To the discerning student it will be readily apparent why both of the above statements are valid.

As we listened to an imaginary reader early in this chapter we assumed that the voice we were hearing might have been either throaty, or nasal, or palatal. That is our introduction to the second rudiment, voice placement. However, before we examine why a voice might be any one of those things, let us try to explain just what is meant by placement.

Voice placement has to do with where the voice is placed in relation to the resonant chambers and resonators. The resonant chambers are the open cavities of the mouth and head, and the resonators are the bony structures of the mouth and face. In this respect, the mouth may be likened to a violin with its sound chamber and its bass bar, sound post, and the surfaces of wood encasing the chamber. The mouth and nasal chamber correspond to the sound chamber of the violin. The hard surfaces correspond to the bass bar, sound post, and so on.

Through voice control it is possible to direct the vocal vibrations of sound into a selected resonant chamber or against a selected resonator. For example, if we confine the voice to the back of the throat we get throaty quality or back placement. In direct contrast, if we throw the voice toward the front of the mouth and bounce the vibrations against the teeth and bony structure of the face, we get a frontal placement.

If we direct the voice still more to the front and take advantage of the teeth as resonators, we get what is called a dental placement. By throwing the voice against the top of the mouth we get a hard-palate placement, and if we let the voice slip slightly farther back, making use of the soft palate, we get a soft-palate placement.

Directing the voice through the nasal chamber gives us a nasal placement, and if we speak from the middle of the mouth we have an oral placement.

The seven basic placements are dental, frontal, oral, back, soft palate, hard palate, and nasal. Any and all of these placements, or any combination of placements may be used effectively for interpretation, but for normal, everyday speech, frontal and oral are the most satisfactory placements because they tend to facilitate clarity of articulation and pleasant tone quality.

Like so many aspects of speech, placement defies accurate written description, but this explanation may stimulate experimentation. It is only through experimentation with the various placements that they can be understood and some mastery of them accomplished. The student should practice each placement, listening carefully to the sound he is producing, as he compares one placement with another. Likewise each student should listen critically to his own normal voice and try to determine what his own predominant placement actually is. If his normal placement is nasal, or back, or hard palate, or soft palate, he will need to practice getting his voice forward. He can do this by focusing his voice toward the front of his face, particularly the areas between the upper lip and the nose. This achieved, he should continue to practice all the placements until he can go from one to another with the greatest of ease.

A recent public reading of Dickens's *A Christmas Carol* was a remarkable model of the use of voice placements in the establishment of the various characters. Old Scrooge, for example, spoke in a growly back placement. When the two solicitors called on the curmudgenous Scrooge for a contribution to charity, one spoke with a nasal placement, the other with a hard-palate placement. The authors of this text have used the placement to establish as many as a dozen different characters in concert readings, and the greatest of all performers of monodrama, the late Ruth Draper, used the art of voice placement with consummate skill.

The third rudiment of reading is *diction*. Naturally we are speaking of diction as it relates to the spoken word rather than diction as an aspect of written rhetoric. In the latter, diction has to do with the selection of words and expressions, whereas in oral reading, as in acting and public speaking, it refers to the way in which words are pronounced and articulated. In this era of the media when strange things are happening to our language, pronunciation and articulation take on a new significance. They have always been important to our own and every language, but in the current bombardment of regional dialects and the onslaught of cross-cultural crossfire, some reevaluation seems in order.

First let us talk about pronunciation. Once there were standards of pronunciation, and those standards were generally accepted by all educated people throughout the English-speaking world. Those standards varied from Webster's *International Standard Dictionary* to Daniel Jones's *English Pronouncing Dictionary*. Perhaps among most well-educated people those standards are still authentic, but the universal corruption of our language is a reality that cannot be ignored. Nor do we use the word *corruption* necessarily in a derogatory sense. The English language has always been in a state of change. It is a language flexible, not fixed. It is that very fact that makes our language vigorous and exciting. It may be that the influence of commercials, the Black community, the hippy cult, the prominence of regional politicians is merely comparable to the color foreign tongues added to the language in times past. In any event, pronunciation, like syntax, is a victim of much diversity. Yet, in the midst of that diversity, we still need standards. Some argue that those standards should come spontaneously from the common public tongue, while others hold that the public tongue is reflected in our dictionaries and that they, the dictionaries, therefore should be our final authority. The altercation must be acknowledged even though it is not one to be settled in this text. Rather let us here agree that pronunciation refers to the way in which a word is spoken according to some acceptable standard. That, for the nonce, is all we need to know.

That is all we need to know anent the controversy, but, practically, it may be helpful to list some of the most common deviations in pronunciation as they are heard in the regions of England and America. Perhaps we should say cultures and classes as well as regions.

Professional readers, like actors, will need to be familiar with the many variations in pronunciation because they are the essence of dialects, and readers and actors are called upon from time to time to perform in diverse dialects. Dialect differs from diction in that it is a departure from a standard whereas diction is an adherence to a standard. However, dialect is a derivative of diction, so is composed of both pronunciation and articulation.

Let us now consider articulation. Articulation, or enunciation, refers to the clarity with which words are spoken. One may articulate perfectly and still have faulty pronunciation, or one may speak with correct pronunciation and still have some degree of careless articulation. One can, but of course one shouldn't. Ideally, we should match articulation with pronunciation.

A simple approach to articulation is the basic understanding of vowels, diphthongs, and consonants. Simple? Only when we can hear the difference in the articulatory sounds and can reproduce those sounds with accuracy. Let us begin, then, with a listing of the fundamental sounds in the English language.

In the following excerpt from Shakespeare's *Hamlet,* most of the sounds most commonly used in English are included.

> Thoughts black, hands apt, drugs fit, and
>   time agreeing;
> Confederate season, else no creature seeing;
> Thou mixture rank, of midnight weeds collected,
> With Hecate's ban thrice blasted, thrice infected,
> Thy natural magic and dire property,
> On wholesome life usurp immediately.
>   William Shakespeare, *Hamlet,* Act III, Scene 2.

In the following sentences, which may be used as articulation drills, virtually all the sounds in the English language are included.

RUDIMENTS OF READING ALOUD / 49

(vowels)
Through the woods and over the water, on and on, and farther and farther—
Truly, should you go on bothering father?
Dewlaps, be it understood, show what honest women are.
Each chilled wet hair lay flat and tight.
We will bet wearily Saturday night.
She will get very saturnine.
A pup is a pup, but a dove is a bird.
Up and up above the herd!
Fill the cup of love with words.

(diphthongs)
They say today's the day they sail away to stay or stray.
Eight maids mating eight mates make eight fateful matings.
Dave, gratefully waiting at the great gate, gave the great gate all the great Dave weight.
Waiting faithfully for her late date, Grace gave her late date the gate.
Friday I fly my kite high in the sky, and that is why my kite and I like Friday fine.
The guys tried frying Heidi, but Heidi fried the guys.
Poised on the hawser, the noisy boys annoy the girls with noisy toys.
Ahoy, ahoy, what joy, what joy, to hoist the sail and sail ahoy!
The oil of Troy is annoyingly oily. Coyly avoid the oil of Troy.
Few knew the news on Tuesday.
The cat may mew and stew in his juice, but he cannot chew his juice or his stew.
They found Dean Brown downtown in his lounging gown!
The counting cow crossed county after county. Now how can a cow count counties?
Around the town the unsound pound is bound to astound.

The above sentences should be read aloud with ears keenly attuned to the subtle differences in the sounds. They will have no value unless they are spoken with definite distinction. This is particularly true of the vowels and diphthongs, which are the singing sounds of the language. Vowels and diphthongs should be spoken with enough duration to give them full value, and students should be warned that it is an all-too-common practice to chop the vowels and diphthongs short, resulting in a staccato speech that does discredit to our language. To illustrate this, read the following poetry, first with a crisp utterance of the vowels and diphthongs, then with a full sustaining of those sounds, noting carefully the difference.

> Stay, O sweet, and do not rise!
> The light that shines comes from thine eyes;
> The day breaks not: it is my heart,
> Because that you and I must part.
> Stay! or else my joys will die
> And perish in their infancy.
>
> John Donne, "Daybreak"

> The ring, so worn as you behold,
> So thin, so pale, is yet of gold:
> This passion such it was to prove—
> Worn with life's care, love yet was love.
>
> George Crabbe, "A Marriage Ring"

Vowels are shaped by the position of the mouth and lips. A demonstration of this can be readily experienced by saying aloud *ooo-eee*. In those two sounds we have the bottom and the top of the vowel scale. The *ooo* sound is at the bottom of the vowel scale and the *eee* is at the top. All other vowels are in between. A full octave range lies between these two vowels, a matter that can be verified by whispering the sounds.

If the *ooo* and the *eee* are uttered correctly, the difference in the shape of the mouth will be strikingly apparent. For the *ooo* the mouth is brought into a puckered position. For the *eee* it is brought into a smiling position. In order to verify this, the vowel and diphthong drills should be done in front of a mirror. Since diphthongs are combinations of vowels, they too should be practiced before a mirror. Of course, the mirror is no substitute for the ear, but it is a valuable assistant.

Let us remember that diphthongs are combinations of two vowels only, and not three. A combination of three vowels is a triphthong. In Cockney dialect, the *I* is spoken as a triphthong, and in Southern dialect the diphthong often becomes a triphthong. Only in dialects are diphthongs permitted to become triphthongs.

The articulation of consonants calls for the use of the tongue as well as the lips. In the formation of such plosive sounds as *p* and *b* and such fricative sounds as *f* and *v* the lips are engaged largely to the exclusion of the tongue, but in such sounds as *l, t,* and *d,* and such sibilants as *s, sh,* and *th,* the tongue plays a major role. It should be observed that the same embouchure position is used for *b* and *p,* the first being voiced, the latter being breathed. Likewise the same position is maintained for *f* and *v,* the first being breathed, the second being voiced. The same is true of *d* and *t*—*d* is voiced, *t* is not.

The consonants that seem to give the most people the most trouble are the *l,* the *s,* the *r,* and the *h,* and the combination of *wh.* *L*'s are often sluggish and not clear because the tongue is not against the upper teeth ridge and curved down instead of up. The *s* sound is often more like an *sh* or a *th.* This can be corrected by saying those three sounds in sequence and working for a slight whistling sound on the *s.* The *r* is often throaty or guttural. This is known as the reflex *r.* We are referring to a mid or final *r* and not an initial *r* or an *r* that is followed by a vowel. The reflex *r* can be adjusted by saying "the world mother" and making the final *r* sound more like *ah* than like the blurry *r*. *H* is often omitted entirely, a custom common in certain British dialects such as Cockney. This habit can be broken by merely giving the *h* more impetus by using more breath. The same principle can improve the articulation of the *wh* in such words as *whisper, white, when,* and so on.

Another common fault in articulation is the failure to sound the final consonant. This is especially noticeable in words that end with *d* or *t,* though it is often true in the case of all words ending with a consonant. A remedy for this is the addition of an *a* sound following the final consonant, a trick used by singers quite consistently. Examples: *let-a* for *let; word-a* for *word, pipe-a* for *pipe,* and the like. However, the best remedy for this and all other articulatory problems is drills, drills, drills. The following sentences contain all the consonants in combinations with all the vowels and diphthongs:

Bab, Babe, Bob, and Bub; each needs a bib when he imbibes like a boob.

To stab a crab in a lab for grub is a flub most drab.

Babbling booby baby Bobbie burped and bubbled in the lobby.

Click, clack, clucks the cuckoo clock ticking in the cloak closet.

Look, look, Uncle Luke, your truck is stuck in the muck!

Koko, the coolie cock, can croak and cluck and kick, and a croaking, clucking, kicking cock is cuckoo.

Dad did a deed the dude died doing.

Don't dawdle, Dora, and do not diddle daddle.

RUDIMENTS OF READING ALOUD / 53

Desperate, determined Dan Dodd dumped a dozen dimes into the duplicator and drew a dud.

Freddie Feifer faithfully fifed on Freddie Feifer's fife, but Feifer found himself fulfilled on Freddie Fiddler's fiddle.

Few folks find fishing fruitful, for few folks fish faithfully.

Fair-feathered friends frequently find friendships fickle, faithless, and fraught with fluff.

A jug generally generates a jag, and jagged gentlemen generally jig and jog gingerly.

Jerry, Joe, and Jack and Margie jilted Jill and Jan and Janie.

Jumping Jupiter! Jolly Jessie Jennifer's Jaguar just generated a general jam.

Giggling girlies gurgling gleefully, gleefully grunt and giggle gurglingly.

They got Gillespie Gunzatto out of the ghetto, but they've not got the ghetto out of Gunzatto.

They've not got garlic in Grandma's glamorous gumbo, but they've got good grunion in Gordie's gorgeous grotto.

Hurry, Harry, hurry! You'll miss the hurley burley!

Into the happy, hallowed, halcyon halls the harrassed hunters hurry, hunting a haven from the hunt, hoping for happiness to have and hold.

Horrendous hordes of hippopotamuses hector human herds while heaven hovers over hordes and herd.

Lil loves to loll by the lilies while Lottie lulls a lullaby.

Lingeringly loitering by lollipops and licorice, lonely little Leota looked longingly, her lips salivating.

Lots of letters fell pell mell while falling hail pelted the mail in the bellowing gale.

"Mum, mam, mum," mumbled Mom, mimicking Mimi Mimmermoss.

Many mighty men make mighty meals of mahi-mahi.

Dames and damsels may damn Miami, but many moola-minded moguls make much of Malibu.

Some dumb bum bummed a drum and doomed the room to gloom.

Nan the nun and Nin the non-nun knew none of the new nun neophytes.

"Ninnie, nannie, nonnie no," sang Nanna nightly in the snow.

Nickeled needles never nestle nicely with nimble noodles, nor nimble noodles neatly with nickeled knives.

In spring each ringing thing will sing "Hey ding-a-ding-a-ding."

Swimming, skiing, boating, and sunning are rollicking things for outing and funning.

Painting, papering, plumbing, and plastering are deviling things for doing and mastering.

Hearing the ringing, singing song of the gong, the sneering, jeering strangers started cheering, proving that tinkling brass can be appealing.

A skunk that cannot drink can't stink, I think, but a mink on the brink of a creek may sink in a chink.

RUDIMENTS OF READING ALOUD / 55

With kinky hair and inky eye, he is a winky, blinky guy.

The clink of each link on the zink of the rink made Pink and Jink slink away.

The peep of Pop with his pipe and the pup on the poop with the Pope was a pip.

Peppy pipers piped peppy ditties while pimply pom pom girlies pranced.

Pupils prosper, purportedly, from poetic purple patches.

A rather rare roar from the rear rather ruptured ruminations.

The ring of rifles from the range ruffles roosters roosting in the rattling rafters.

The hours in the tower are our hours, are they not?

In the merriment the fairies carried Harry to the carriage.

The hurry and flurry was quite a worry, but the marriage of Mary was very merry.

I'm sorry the hoary old lorry is so horribly gory.

The saucy songs of Dr. Seuss are sassy sauce for sons and Sis.

Suspecting his suspenders were slipping, his suspicion sustained the suspense.

Salty Sam and sugary Bea seasoned supper scrumptiously.

Ship shape and sharp, Shorty shall surely ship out shortly.

Sheila shines shells on the shiny, shelly shore, shaking shells from shale, as she shivers like a sheep shunning shelter.

Lush as a dish of fresh fish hash is a ration of mish mash mush.

The tot can toot, and tote, and trot, and that's a lot for a tiny, tooting, toting, trotting tot.

It takes twelve tranquil tenders, all taking tranquilizers, to tend ten tiny teeter totters teetering twenty tiny teeter totterers.

It might be trite to fight the night with light, but trite or or not it is quite right.

Theta thimbles her thumbs when thumbing through thistles.

Thin, thorough Thelma threaded through the thickening, thrilling throng.

Although Methuselah may have enthused the throngs, he was as disenthralled as a misanthrope.

Vitality is the valve of verve and verve the vortex of vivacity.

The vivid view that Vivian viewed virtually vibrated with verisimilitude.

Voulez, voulez, voulez-vous, swerve to curve the village view?

When Winthrop Winter went to woo, he went in winter weather, yet Winthrop Winter won a wife in weather wet for wooing.

While wallowing wantonly in Walla Walla waters, we wondered why and what it was we wanted.

Unwashed, unwanted, and unwed, she showered and scoured her bowed, unworthy head.

Whether it's whither or whether it's whence, it's always where, and while, and when.

While whispering white lies, which white lie was whispered?

Whether the weather is warm or wet, I whet my wit while waiting away.

Yeah, yeah, ye youthful yelling yellow yeomen, your yell is young and yielding.

Yon youthful yappers and yon young yippers are yet too young to yearn for Yom Kippurs.

You-all yearning to be yawning aboard that Yankee yawl yonder?

Does the cruise you choose ooze with booze, and does a buzzard buzz at the fuzz on a fez?

The zephyr zeroed in on Xerxes observing a dozen zany zebras snoozing among zithers and xylophones.

Sizzling dizzily, Zora zoomed in on the zealous Xanthippe with a dazzling zing.

(Sibilants)

See Shirley's thumb.

See Cheryl's thimble.

Simply shoot thrice.

Sing short themes.

Sister shall thirst.

As will be discovered later, if it isn't already apparent, diction is a rudiment that must be mastered with some degree of proficiency if reading is to be communicated.

No one is likely to be interested in listening to somebody read if he cannot understand what the reader is saying. Therefore, the student is urged to take the above drills and exercises seriously and work on them rigorously and consistently.

The next rudiment to be discussed is projection. Clear diction and a pleasing voice are of limited value unless both are adequately projected. Public address systems compensate for a lack of projection as they accommodate modern readers and speakers, but with or without microphones, projection is a reading rudiment with which we needs must cope. Coping with microphones calls for one technique; coping without them calls for another.

With the advent of electronic amplification, projection has reached a sorry plight. Not that amplification should be always spurned. On the contrary, it is one of the marvels of the times and can be used to great advantage. Nevertheless, it is a sad comment on the modern human voice when a speaker system has to be turned on every time there is a committee meeting. Today, it seems every time an individual is to address a handful of people it is assumed that he will need a microphone. Actually, the microphone has become a kind of status symbol, but it is an insult to anyone who has had voice training. Anyone with training can make himself heard even in a rather spacious auditorium without the distorting benefit of amplification. We say "distorting" because the human voice is often made to sound much worse over the speaker system than it actually is. However, the voice need not be distorted by a sound system, so let us give some thought to the mechanical aspect of projection. In those instances where amplification is necessary or desirable, certain procedures and precautions should be taken into account.

If microphones are to be used, they should be used to the best possible advantage. The microphones, the power amplifier, and the loudspeakers are there to help, not to hinder. It is the function of a sound system to aid the auditory reception of the audience and show the speaker or performer at his best. Final control of this lies largely in the hands of the sound technician who, unfortunately in all too many cases, may be an overworked custodian with no knowledge of electronics or acoustics. Therefore it is incumbent upon the performer to check the sound system in advance wherever possible. When feasible, the performer will be wise to test the system before the audience arrives and, if possible, have a friend check his voice from various parts of the auditorium.

Many people nowadays have at least some elementary mike training, but a few reminders may be in order. First, no one should ever work too close to the microphone. Doing so tends to garble the articulation rather than enhance it. Also, in some systems the low frequencies boom out like tympani. Best results are usually achieved by working about a foot or eighteen inches from the mike. Extraneous sounds, such as rattling the pages of a script, turn into virtual sound effects when amplified, so they should be avoided. A lavaliere mike hung about the neck is often very satisfactory, but one must take care that clothing does not rub against the mike and that it is not placed where inhalation is picked up audibly. These pointers may be embarrassingly obvious to some, but they are mentioned because it is astonishing to discover how many people do not know the simplest rules regarding the use of microphones.

Now let us leave the microphones for those occasions when they must be used and talk about voice projection.

Projection is not shouting. That is the first fact to recognize. A whisper can be projected. That is the second fact to realize. What, then, is projection?

Simply stated, projection is speaking to the people in the back row in a voice that sounds normal and conversational. It is using voice placement to direct the voice to the desired area. This means using breath support and speaking on the breath.

However, projection is something more. More than voice must get back to those people in the back row. Thoughts must get through to them. Feelings must get through to them. Ideas must get through to them. Thoughts, feelings, and ideas must be transmitted in order to trigger their thoughts, feelings, and ideas. How can this be done? By thinking and by caring. In addition to the vocal technique mentioned above, it is necessary to "think" what you are saying as you say it, and will your way into the ears and mind and heart of every spectator by your sheer desire to reach them. Projection is psychological as well as vocal.

For those who have trouble with projection, here are a few suggestions. Belt out the following words until they seem to bounce back from the rear wall: hook, hoak, hank, hunk. Listen to the sound of your voice as you do this and try to get the feel of the projection in your mouth and chest. Next, talk to somebody in the rear of the auditorium. Carry on a conversation with him. Have him ask you questions, the answers to which you must get across to him. Now trade places with that person and let him take the stage and you go to the rear of the auditorium. In those positions continue your conversation. Keep this up until it is easy and natural to talk across the existing space. Another helpful trick is to pretend your best friend is seated in the last row over in a corner. Rehearse a segment of your performance with that friend in mind, remembering that it is that friend you want to reach. In all of these experiments, listen! Grow accustomed to the sound of your own voice in relation to the acoustics of the room. Make it a point to fill the whole room with your voice. Take vocal command of the space.

Presence is our next rudiment. Some people seem to have been born with stage presence, but everyone can acquire a degree of it—everyone who really wants it and is willing to work for it. It is something eminently worth working for. Without it, public appearance is impractical. No one without presence is likely to make much of an impression on a public gathering of any kind.

Stage fright is a mortal enemy to presence. We do not mean the kind of stage fright that manifests itself in that hollow feeling in the pit of the stomach just before an entrance. That kind of stage fright is good and should be cultivated. That brand of stage fright is the kind professionals pray they will never lose. There should always be that tingle of excitement, that tummy full of butterflies, just before the big moment comes. That is the friendly fright, the one that helps, and not the terrifying one that hinders.

The hindering kind of stage fright is a basic fear of failure. It reveals itself in shyness, lack of projection, self-abasement, excessive alibis; or in contrast, sometimes in bluster, clowning, and diverse efforts toward ego building. The first step toward developing presence is the acquiring of proficiency in the rudiments discussed above. The second step is to overcome the fear of failure. Interestingly enough, the first contributes to the second. Proficiency in technique is the finest bulwark against fear.

However, there is a sure-fire formula for knocking the fear of failure into the proverbial cocked hat. The formula can be best presented in a few forthright questions. Here they are: Who are you that you shouldn't fail? What's so special about you? Why shouldn't you fail? You aren't God, are you?

The facing frankly of such hard questions gets at the psychological quirk that causes fear of failure. Once that quirk is yanked out like a bad tooth, an amazing reversal usually takes place. Once the student realizes that immediate perfection is not expected of him; that some failures, in fact, are most definitely expected; that he, like everyone else in the business, will make mistakes, he will be well on his way to acquiring presence.

It is through failure that we learn and grow. We make mistakes, stumble, fall flat, pick ourselves up, try again, fail again, correct that error, and go on from there. It is through the very process of making mistakes and correcting them that success is won. Most of us have to knock down a lot of hurdles before we learn to clear them, but if we realize that we will have to knock them down before we master them, we can work with freedom.

Freedom is the essence of presence. When we are free we are confident, and what is presence if it isn't an innate self-confidence? It may be other things, of course. It may be dewy-eyed enthusiasm, it may be and often is a kind of magnetism, and even, at times, an actual charisma; but fundamentally presence is the dominion of self-confidence.

The final rudiment is *communication*. Thus far we have been dealing in the main with the physical and psychological aspects of reading. Communication carries us into the realm of the intellect. Not that there are not physical and mechanical aspects of communication. There are, and we shall deal with them extensively in the ensuing chapter on interpretation. However, the rudiment of communication is the last, for which all the other rudiments were precursors, and we must now apply the mechanics and techniques to the primordial point.

Why do we read aloud, if not to communicate? Why do we fuss about voice, diction, projection, and presence, and why must those rudiments be studied and practiced, if not to communicate? If we do not communicate we are huffing and puffing for so much sound and fury, and our audience may as well have stayed home. In order to communicate, we need all the techniques discussed above, but we need also an intellectual understanding of the content we are attempting to communicate.

Finally, we need to have some mastery of the tools of interpretation in order to complete the job of communicating. However, the whole matter of interpretation has such significance that we shall devote the following chapter to it. These are the rudiments of reading. Now let us consider the elements of interpretation.

3

The Elements of Interpretation

The elements of interpretation are nothing more nor less than the tools of the trade. They are the devices by which we convey the meaning of content or express our thoughts to others. They are the vocal media which we use daily in conversation as well as in reading, acting, or speech making. Therefore the elements of interpretation are not strangers, because we use one or more of them each time we speak. Yet the curious thing about the elements is the fact that we seldom stop to think about them and therefore do not always use them wisely; or, in all too many cases, misuse them or fail to make them do what they are designed to do, which is to convey meaning.

It is because of their misuse or inadequate use that we must take time to study the elements. We have said that they are not strangers, yet, although we use them constantly, some of them will no doubt appear as strangers. This is because few people have taken the time to analyze the elements and thereby clear up the confusion that hangs over them. For example, one element is often confused with another. Pitch, for instance, is confused with melody, and rhythm with tempo or rate. Pause, or caesura, gets mixed up with phrasing or rhythm, or, as we shall call it, rubato.

Let us begin with the element called *stress*. First let us clarify what stress is not. Stress is not the same as accent, and it is not the same as emphasis. Accent, in our parlance, refers to the syllable of a word. The accent may be on the first syllable or on the second syllable or on some other syllable of a word. In the word *accent,* for example, the accent is on the first syllable. In the word *defeat* the accent is on the second syllable. Emphasis, in our theory, refers to a segment of content. Key phrases that define a story line, for instance, must be given emphasis, and emphasis must be given the climax, and so on.

Stress, on the other hand, refers to the word which must be given special importance. In the sentence "All men believe in something," we can stress the words *all* and *something*. In that case the meaning that would be conveyed should be that everyone, though he may not believe as another, does believe in something. If, on the other hand, we should stress the words *men* and *believe,* we would imply that all men, though not necessarily women and children, are believers.

Thus we see that stress conveys both explicit and implicit meaning. We will find this to be true of other elements as well, but stress is one of the most obvious of the elements and therefore one of the most dynamic. By way of further illustration, read the following sentences, stressing the words that appear in upper case type.

1a. (Improper stress) WE gave the report TO the com-

mittee, and AFTER weeks of delay, we GOT no action, AND had to settle FOR virtually nothing.
1b. (Proper stress) WE gave the report to the COMMITTEE, and, after WEEKS of DELAY, we got no action, and had to SETTLE for virtually NOTHING.

2a. (Improper stress) MANY people say MANY things which mean nothing to MANY people.
2b. (Proper stress) Many PEOPLE say many THINGS which mean NOTHING to many people.

3a. (Improper stress) How can we WHIP inflation with everybody WANTING more money?
3b. (Proper stress) HOW can we whip INFLATION with everybody wanting more MONEY?

4a. (Improper stress) Let us be silent a WHILE and LET the glory AND the love of God WHOLLY possess us.
4b. (Proper stress) Let us be SILENT a while, and let the love and glory of GOD wholly POSSESS us.

5a. (Improper stress) She went WITH the manager TO the checker and made out a check for the groceries.
5b. (Proper stress) She went with the MANAGER to the CHECKER and made out a CHECK for the groceries.

Note in the above sentences how a change in stress invariably connotes a change in meaning. Note, too, how a faulty stress can distort the meaning. Faulty stresses are a common handicap to interpretation, so need to be eradicated. A first step to interpretation is the discovery of the inevitable stresses—that is to say, the right stresses.

In common with faulty stressing is the practice of overstressing. Many people have the habit of stressing too many words. The whole value of the stress is lost if stress is used excessively. As a general rule the average sentence calls for two stresses, a primary and a secondary. Stressing each and every word in a sentence would be like singing a song with all the notes given equal value in terms of dynamics. Yet the average inexperienced reader does just that. The result is a failure to convey meaning and a pattern that is dull and monotonous.

Stress may be effected by a variation in volume, or in pitch, or in duration. Stress through volume is achieved through giving the stressed word an extra thrust of vocal power or by reducing the vocal power and speaking the stressed word with sudden softness, thus achieving stress through a contrast in dynamics. In musical terminology this sort of adumbration would be signified by a fortissimo sign, *ff,* or by a symbol of pianissimo, *pp*. A stress by means of pitch can also be compared to music. As is the case with volume, the key to stress is contrast. A word may be stressed by speaking it higher in pitch from the other words of the sentence, or by saying it lower than the rest of the sentence. We may also use musical nomenclature in defining stress by duration. Here the time value of the various notes can be compared with the duration of the stressed word. For example, the unstressed words might be marked with eighth notes and the stressed words with quarter or half notes.

Students who read music can be greatly aided in their understanding of the elements of interpretation by marking their texts with musical symbols. Later we will illustrate how this can be done, but the illustration will have more significance when we have considered the other elements of interpretation. Meanwhile, let us borrow another musical term to help us with our next element.

The word is *rubato*. It is akin to phrasing in verbal composition. In music, it is the stealing of time from some notes in order to give more time to others. A measure of music consisting of four beats, for instance, might have two eighth notes, one quarter note, and a half note. In singing or playing the measure in strict time, we would give the exact value to each note, but to sing or play it with rubato, we would shorten ever so slightly the time value of the eighth and quarter notes, and add that borrowed time to the half note. Why would we do this? We would do it to give the music more meaning, more style, and more variety. That is precisely what rubato does in oral interpretation.

A phrase or a sentence that is read with each and every word getting the same time value is not very interesting, nor does it contribute much toward conveying meaning nor suggest any sort of flair. It is, in fact, deadly dull, yet such reading is uncomfortably common. It is the kind of reading most usually heard from inexperienced or untrained readers. The close relation of rubato to stress is as significant as it is apparent. They are related for a good cause. They help each other. Rubato contributes directly to stress and stress is the peak point of rubato. In rubato words are clustered together much as flowers are assembled in an artistic floral arrangement. Each floral arrangement has a focal point and each cluster of words has a stress.

Another near relative to stress is *pause*. It, too, is akin to rubato. In fact, we might say that pause is the hiatus between phrases, and it is the rubato that makes a phrase sound like a phrase. Pause is the stop, the time lag, the instant of silence, the caesura that prevents the words that are spoken from being a jangle of uninterrupted sound.

The importance of the pause is apparent, but its effective use is mercilessly underrated. As has been said of the symphonies of Beethoven, the most exalting music is in the moments of silence which are indicated in the score by a pause. The interruption of sound by silence can be profound. So there is great power in the pause.

Naturally, the duration of pauses varies vastly. Some are long, some short. There is the almost imperceptible pause that contributes to the clarity of articulation, that tiny fraction of time between words sometimes referred to as a breath gap. There is the catch-breath pause which is slightly longer, being only long enough for the quick inhalation of sufficient breath. There is the cadence pause that comes at the end of a statement. Similar to that is the interrogatory pause which follows a question, and the exclamatory pause which follows an exclamation point. Finally, there is the dramatic pause which must be long enough to give the audience an opportunity to feel the full impact of suspense or the total reality of the situation.

Rubato has a first cousin called *melody*. The truth is, all the interpretive elements are close kin. Melody is so often confused with rubato that we might conclude that they are twin cousins. Yet, as we shall see, they are clearly distinguishable elements, and melody plays quite a different role from that of rubato.

Melody is what melody always is—a tune. In oral interpretation, the tune may not always be particularly musical, but it is a tune, nonetheless. It is a tune even when it is rendered in the drone of a monotone. Actually, we usually think of monotone as a lack of melody, and we think wisely, but as an interpretive element we have to consider even a drone a melody of a kind.

Melody is sometimes mistaken for another of her relatives known as *pitch*, but actually they are not alike, as we shall see when we get acquainted with pitch. They do have something in common, because they are both married to the musical scale. However, melody runs all over the musical scale, or at least has that prerogative. The drone, of course, does not exercise that prerogative, though certainly any drone-prone reader should.

Melody relates to the many variations in pitch within a paragraph, a sentence, a phrase, or even a single word. Where there is wide variation, a quantity of melody is being used. Where there is little or no variation, the melody is slight. That drone again!

Some roles and some readings call for a great deal of melody, while others call for very little. The amount of melody to be employed is determined by such things as the nature and style of the content, the amount and kind of impersonation, and the presentational concept. Smart, sophisticated comedy is likely to call for a great deal of melody, whereas the artisans in Shakespeare's *A Midsummer Night's Dream* would use much less.

We should raise aloft two words of warning about melody. The words are *phoniness* and *repetition*. Melody must ring true. Phony melodies result in an unbelievable performance. The reader must say with pitch variation what the words are written to say. Any melody that is not indigenous to the line or sentence is certain to be artificial.

Repetitious melodies are common among amateurs. They find themselves in a rut, and read everything with the same melody. Each sentence has the same sing-song inflection. *Inflection*. That is the word that is often used when people mean melody, but in our terminology inflection is a more general term and melody is but one element. Inflection or melody, repetitious patterns should be broken by deliberate exercises in melody variation. There are drills ahead that will help.

Pitch, that kinsman to melody we promised to introduce, can best be explained as the key in which a given passage or a certain scene is read. Pitch is the musical signature of the performance. A reader may use many keys in the course of his presentation, but each is relative to the other.

There may be many and various melodies delivered in a certain pitch, and those same melodies may be read exactly the same in another pitch, which is a way of saying that pitch is an element unto itself and has little, but only little, in common with melody.

Nick Bottom, in Shakespeare's *A Midsummer Night's Dream,* may play all his scenes in the low pitch of a basso profundo, and Flute, impersonating Thisbe, may play everything in a high falsetto. In such an extreme we have a good example of pitch. A reader presenting a program of poetry may read some poems in a low key and others in a high key, and he may set each piece of verse in a distinctive key. On the other hand, he may choose to change from one pitch to another within a single poem. The choice of pitch, or pitches, is a fairly arbitrary matter, except that pitch, like all the other elements, is to be used to interpret, not merely to create an effect.

If tempo has any close kin among the elements, the kinsman is rubato, and we might say that tempo and rubato are related in somewhat the same way that melody and pitch are. Rubato, as we have discovered, relates to cluster, or phrases. Tempo relates to a much larger quantity of the performance. Tempo consists of the number of words that are spoken in a given length of time. A reader may deliver his presentation in a slow, deliberate tempo, or at a rate resembling the firing of a machine gun. That word *rate* gives us the key to tempo. It is a synonym.

Tempo may refer to a total performance or to various segments of that performance. A reader may, and usually does, employ a variety of tempi in his presentation. If he is interpreting a number of characters, each character can be established by a particular tempo. Narrative material, too, may be given variety by altering the rate of delivery. Poetry is often read at a slower tempo than prose; however, this is more a guideline than a rule. Verse should be read at a rate slow enough for the audience to get the value of the vowel sounds, but certainly some verse is more effective when taken at a rapid clip. The nature of the content determines the tempo. Nevertheless, tempo is not a thing that should be left to chance. A reader should set his tempi in advance as part of his preparation, very much as a pianist does when he is preparing a concert.

Although we need not treat it as a separate element, we should give some consideration to the word *rubato*. It refers to the length of a word, a syllable, or a vowel. For that matter, it refers also to the length of a pause. A pause might be held for the duration of three or four beats. A vowel might be sustained for the duration of a whole note, a half note, or a quarter note. A word can be chopped or sustained, according to the desired duration. Vowels in lyrical or romantic passages should be sustained; giving the vowel sounds suitable duration adds to the lyrical quality of the material.

In this discussion of tempo the words *legato* and *staccato* merit some attention. The sustaining of vowels in a relatively slow tempo creates a legato effect. On the other hand, cutting the duration of each sound crisply creates an effect that is called *staccato*. When a reader employs staccato where legato should be observed, he is in trouble, and the reverse is equally true. This may seem obvious until someone attempts to read a Shakespearean sonnet or a scene from one of Shakespeare's plays. It is safe to estimate that nine out of ten untrained readers will chop their words in an abominable staccato when they attempt to read lyrical verse. On the other hand, the prolongation of vowels and diphthongs in a passage that should move rapidly results in a tedium that is equally abhorrent. Suit the tempo and the aspects of the tempo to the content. That is the objective.

We come now to the element of dynamics, the softness and loudness of the business. This is the element that is measured by the degree of volume, and for that reason is probably the one most readily understood. "Do you want it soft or loud?" One might assume that an answer to that question would settle the matter. However, there's a little more to be said about dynamics.

We need to say, for instance, that there is a wide range of dynamics available to a reader; a range which, without training, he is not likely to utilize to fullest advantage. As everyone familiar with music knows, there is a vast difference between a triple *ppp* (piano, pianissimo) and a triple *fff* (forte, fortissimo). A reader can make use of just such a range if he trains himself to do so. He can begin by training his ear to hear not merely the difference between soft and loud but all the subtle shadings of the dynamics that lie between the two extremes. He can begin by reciting the alphabet, first in a whisper, then gradually, very gradually, louder and louder until he reaches the peak of a comfortable volume. Notice, we say *comfortable volume*. Nothing is ever to be gained by forcing a volume that is beyond the reader's tonal capacity. He may expand that capacity, but he must do it gradually.

As with the other elements, the element of dynamics is to be used to give a performance variety, interest, and interpretive values. It is an element to be used with a knowledge of crescendo and decrescendo. Crescendo, another term conveniently borrowed from the nomenclature of music, means a gradual increase in volume. The use of crescendo is an excellent device for creating variety. It is also a handy device for the handling of nuances, but let us save the element of nuance for the last.

Intensity is an element that is understood best through experience. We can define it somewhat inadequately as quantitative emotion. It is measured by the amount of emotion that is communicated in a word, a phrase, or a passage.

We should add that intensity has a second meaning that is more easily explained. Intensity refers to the amount of vitality that is expressed in a performance or at various moments in a performance. It is expressed through vocal vibrance, facial mobility, and most especially in the expression in the eyes. Vitality includes such things as verve and veracity. That word "veracity" helps to tie together the two meanings of intensity.

Implicit in quantitative emotion is quality as well. Intensity calls for integrity of emotion and honesty of thought. It is not merely that inner motivation advocated by Stanislavski. Rather, it is that inner motivation expressed with zest.

It may be that the fourteenth-century Japanese actor and theorist Zeami was thinking in terms of intensity when he wrote his famous words about *yugen*.

In teaching young actors, Zeami talked a great deal about *yugen* which, admittedly, is a difficult word to translate. Several meanings are implicit, but those that seem to come through clearest are these: the overtones of subtlety; the subliminal as opposed to the obvious; the essence beneath the surface; the internal truth that lies beneath the external expression; and a basic grace and beauty. Apparently he was saying something to the effect that *Whatever you do, make it significant and make it beautiful.* In terms of intensity, we might define *yugen* as the "harmonics of the content." The idea is to bring to the audience something more than the words, even something more than the ideas. The reader, like the actor, should suggest more than the lines alone convey.

The penultimate element is *quality*. A quick reference to our discussion of voice placement from the preceding chapter should help to explain what we mean by quality. However, the many and various vocal qualities which a reader should be able to produce are only part of what we mean by quality. We do mean vocal qualities, of course, such as guttural, nasal, breathy, and the like. However, quality as an element of interpretation goes beyond the use of vocal techniques, important as it is. Quality includes the use of phonetics, but goes beyond this, too.

Before we go further, however, let us reaffirm that voice and movement do have a lot to do with quality. In this respect we think of quality as it refers to the overall presentation as well as to the components of that presentation. In other words, we think of quality, vocal and phonetic, as it is used in the expression of thought, emotion, and idea. Such is certainly a major function of quality. However, quality has another attribute which, though more abstract, is nonetheless relevant and fascinating.

That attribute is the extra ingredient which makes the difference between excellence and mediocrity. It is the dreamed-of, hoped-for goal, the unreachable star, which on those rare high moments is reached and realized. Zeami had a word for it. The word is *hana*. Translated literally, the word means "flower," but *hana* is no ordinary flower. It is something rare, strange, unexpected. It is the surprise element in a performance. It is that something which makes an audience feel it is getting its money's worth and more. It is the professional "plus" that a performer experiences in his performance. To the performer, *hana* is the bursting into bloom of a talent well cultivated. To the audience, it is an extension of an adventure that goes beyond the thing that was expected.

The final element is *nuance*. Nuance is the slight, subtle, delicate deviation that gives dimension to meaning and professional status to the performance. The other elements converge in nuance to refine and give finesse.

At the heart of nuance is the dramatic build. The elements unite through technical control to give the content ebb and flow. It is the ebb and flow that enunciate the peaks and valleys. The peaks are minor climaxes, all of which must lead to the inevitable ultimate climax.

Since the build is the heart of nuance, let us examine the structure of a build. A build can be accomplished through the use of several elements, or through the use of one single element. The amateur, who is often not aware of his diverse possibilities, usually tries unconsciously to get all his build by using all the elements. That is to say, he uses all the elements that can be naturally combined to get a build. For example, he is likely to use volume, pitch, tempo, emphasis, and even stress, all thrown together indiscriminately. This combination is not to be ruled out, because it can be thoroughly effective, but its effectiveness wears thin with excessive repetition. The well-trained reader knows he can achieve a build merely by increasing his volume. He can also get a build by raising his pitch, or by speeding up the tempo, or by playing with increasing intensity. He can also get a build by adding extra stresses, or by punching his stresses with extra force. He can achieve a build by using any one of these elements singly, quite independent of the others.

Similarly, a build can be achieved through a combination of volume and pitch, or through a combination of pitch and tempo, or through a combination of tempo and volume, or by combining intensity with any one of those elements. In other words, a build can be the product of one single element, or it can be the product of two elements, or the product of a combination of three or more elements.

The elements of interpretation as we have been considering them are largely of an organic, physiological, and mechanical nature. This is only natural, since we are treating them as tools and devices to be used in the interest of performance perfection. It is only by becoming aware of and familiar with such tools that we can begin to use them effectively. Until we do learn how to use them as performance techniques, we are left in a limbo of amateurism and are limited to a kind of intuitive trial-and-error approach, for the dominion over the trial-and-error method may be enhanced by a knowledge of kinetics.

4

Kinetics, the Visual Aspects of Oral Interpretation

Seeing is hearing. Absurd? The statement may seem so, but as we shall soon see, it has considerable validity.

In a dramatic performance, even the slightest movement will steal the focus of the audience from an actor who is statically delivering lines. Let the actor cease to be static and augment what he is saying with a gesture, and the focus goes back to him. Action does speak louder than words. However, we are writing about the spoken word, not about the art of pantomime. How can the spoken word be seen? How can something that is being read be received through visual response?

This chapter purports to answer those questions. That they must be answered is, in fact, the motivation for this chapter. Probably everyone who reads this text is thorougly aware of the importance of gestures. However, the acknowledgment of the importance of gestures is not the same as the fascinating world of kinetics. That world is happily much vaster than the uninitiated may realize. It offers far more than a few hackneyed gestures and overworked facial expressions. It is a world which dancers, pantomimists, and actors have been exploring for centuries, yet with areas still to be explored. As we explore, let us keep in mind the opening statement of this chapter, "seeing is hearing." Let us also remember that action speaks louder than words and see how that fact makes the tasteful, discriminating use of gestures imperative.

First let us dispose of a controversy or two which might conceivably get in our way. There are those who believe that little if any movement or facial expression is necessary in the art of oral interpretation. Advocates of this viewpoint usually are the ones who make a sharp distinction between oral interpretation and acting, and insist that a reading should be a reading and not a performance. Usually they carry this conviction to the point of insisting that the reader actually read from his manuscript rather than make his presentation from memory. In their judgment memorization defeats the basic idea of a public reading. This is a legitimate viewpoint worthy of respect, and may well be the best approach for some readers.

The opposite position holds that oral interpretation calls for all of the interpretive skills that are applicable and that dependence on voice alone is altogether too limiting. Tantamount to this position is the conviction that the basic idea of public reading is the communication of content, and in order to do that many techniques are called for.

It may be argued that the first viewpoint is easier and makes fewer demands on the reader and therefore calls for much less training. This may be true, although the supporters of the viewpoint could probably present a sound rebuttal. In any event, we shall not quibble about the two postures. It is enough to acknowledge the controversy and get on with the presentation of techniques that may be helpful to either viewpoint, though obviously more helpful to those who take the latter position.

Actually, it is impossible to ignore completely the visual aspects of oral reading unless the reading is a radio broadcast, in which case an interesting reversal of the "seeing is hearing" theory occurs. In radio we have a perfect example of the contention that hearing is seeing. So it is. All of which leads to a conclusion which serves as a springboard for the dive we are about to take into kinetics. The conclusion can be stated in the word *imagination*. The unseen reader on the air must reach the imagination of his listeners. When he does, they see what they hear. That is, they see the images which the words suggest. Conversely, the viewer's visual sense triggers his imagination when the reader augments what he is reading by suiting the action to the word.

To carry out Hamlet's advice and "suit the action to the word and the word to the action" is to open a wide gateway to the imagination. If the action is not suited to the word it is pointless and better omitted altogether. The action, the gesture, or the facial expression must enhance, augment, enliven, or enrich the text if it is to have impact on the imagination of the audience. Visual expressions can confuse, distort, and even contradict when they are not suitable and right.

How do we know when they are suitable and right? Some know intuitively. They are the fortunate ones. However, even intuition is on safer grounds when it is backed up with sound theory. That there is sound theory governing action is a fact that some people have known for centuries. Yet, old though it is, it is far from universal knowledge. Through the centuries the theory has been identified in various ways, but we call it, simply, visual dynamics.

Visual dynamics are a veritable insurance policy for those who work intuitively, a sure-fire substitute to those who are lacking in intuition. It is a kind of security, a system for double checking on the suiting of the action to the word. It is a system that has been used both consciously and, by intuitive artists, unconsciously since the days of classical Greece and probably long before. It has been used by balladeers, dancers, pantomimists, actors, and even priests through the ages. Visual dynamics are apparent in the work of great choreographers, good orators, well-directed dramatic productions, and in the celebration of the Catholic mass.

Like phonic dynamics, visual dynamics are based on strength and weakness. "Do you want it loud or soft?" In the realm of the visual that question becomes "should it be strong or weak?" Every movement is either one or the other. Every action is either accentuating or diminishing. As in the case of sound, there are variations between the extremes. Every action does not have the same degree of strength or weakness. One movement may be very strong, another not quite so strong, and so on, but basically all movement is either strong or weak.

A categorization of strong and weak movements might go something like this: To stand is strong; to sit is weak. To lift the head, chin up, is strong; to bow the head is weak. The raising of an arm or both arms is strong as compared to letting the arms fall to the side. In terms of basic gestures, about which there will be more later, the punch, or thrust, the slash, the lift, would all be strong. The fall, the glide, the rub, or shuffle are weak. A full-front body position (facing the audience) is strong, as is a one-quarter right or one-quarter left position. Turning away from the audience to a profile position or to a three-quarter position is obviously weak, although a full-back position is relatively strong because it is stronger than either profile or the closed three-quarter position. Moving toward the audience is strong. Moving away from it is weak. Moving from stage left to stage right is strong. The reverse is weak. Stage right and left, it must be remembered, is from the actor's viewpoint when he is facing the audience.

If the above listing of strong and weak movements seems arbitrary, a careful testing of each movement and gesture will soon reveal that the listing is thoroughly valid. In fact, it is only through experiencing and observing these movements and gestures that validity can be fully established. However abstract the theory of visual dynamics may appear, it is a theory that is based upon empirical knowledge, and each student must experience for himself the movements described above if he is to acquire a working knowledge of the theory.

Actually, the difference between a strong and weak movement is usually so apparent that no one should have much difficulty getting the hang of it. The only one that might not be immediately apparent is the lateral movement from left to right and vice versa. This can be best tested through observation. Even then it is safe to estimate that one out of fifty will disagree with the theory. In many classes through many years we have discovered that there are always a few who cannot see a marked difference between a movement from stage left to stage right and from stage right to left. However, the mavericks do not necessarily disprove the theory. What they do prove is that no theory is ever finally and forever fixed. All theories are open to question. Nevertheless, here is a theory that can be taken hold of and the odds in favor of its feasibility are better than a thousand to one. In any event, no theory should be disregarded until it has been disproved.

The next step is the application of visual dynamics to the text that is to be presented. We know what movements are strong, what actions are weak, but how do we suit the action to the word? The text tells us. A study of the contents reveals a similar scale of dynamics in terms of strength and weakness. Words, phrases, sentences—all have their own dynamics. Some are strong, some are weak.

To read a strong line such as "I stand here on my conviction, and from this position I will not budge," for example, and accompany the reading with a weak movement like turning away from the audience and bowing the head would be so obviously incongruous that it would produce a laugh from the audience. Or to read "The culprit knew when he was trapped and gave up quietly" with a raising of the head and a gesture toward the ceiling would be equally ridiculous.

However, these selected lines are obvious in terms of suiting the action to the word. Here are a few random lines presented, first with no suggested gestures, then repeated with what could well be suitable action.

For the following sentences, suitable accompanying action is given first, followed by incorrect action.

1. "Now I would like to made a direct appeal to each and all of you."
    a. Take a step or two toward the audience for a more intimate contact.
    b. Back up a step or two moving away from the audience.
2. "Confident of these ideals, I embrace the world."
    a. Arms up and open in an embracing gesture.

b. Hands folded across stomach with fingers interlocked.
3. "On this conviction I stand firm. What does the opposition propose to do about it?"
    a. Arms folded and chin up.
    b. Hands limp at the sides and chin down.
4. "Frankly, I would punch every character like that in the nose."
    a. Thrust clenched fist forward on the words "punch" and "nose."
    b. Tap fingers of right hand in palm of left hand in casual manner.
5. "Every dollar that came in only heightened his miserly greed."
    a. Rub hands together in front of the chest.
    b. Stand with hands on hips, arms akimbo.

The above directions are merely meant to indicate how the action might be suited to the word, and certainly must not suggest that other directions might not be selected. Every reader should work out his own pattern of action. The important thing is that he should be able to distinguish between the strong and weak lines. This should not be particularly difficult if he remembers that dynamics are always related to the communication of the content. However, it is obvious that a thorough understanding of the text is basic. Aids to understanding will be discussed in a later chapter.

It is important to point out at this time that the student should not conclude that all action is limited to visual dynamics. Visual dynamics are merely a part of the major techniques, but let us hasten to add that there are other techniques, such as the manipulation of the basic gestures.

By basic gestures we do not mean a kind of sign language such as was worked out years ago by Delsarte. For all its merits, the Delsarte method proved to be much too artificial. It belonged to the era of elocution, and the practice of the method passed out of fashion along with the passing of elocution. While it is true that we may salvage from Delsarte the things that were good about the system—things which will pop up later in our discussion of pantomimic details—the basic gestures we want to talk about are as natural as they are basic. They are the universal gestures that are common to practically all peoples everywhere. Thrust, for example, is a gesture anyone may make when he pounds one fist into the palm of the other hand, or slaps a hand on a table, or punches a point with a forefinger. Any sudden projection by a hand, an arm, an elbow, the chin, a knee, or a foot would be considered a thrust. A kick, for example, is a thrust. So is a punch in the nose, not that many such punches are likely called for in the average reading.

Akin to the thrust is the slash. When Hamlet said "Nor do not saw the air too much with your arms thus," he was talking about the slash. That word *sawing* gives us the key to the slash. In contrast to the sudden, impulsive movement of the thrust, the slash is a little more gradual. He might slash with a sword, whereas he would thrust with a fencing foil. He would slash with a golf club, but thrust with a boxing glove. In football, a punt is a thrust and a pass is a slash.

If we do a slash in slow motion, we have a glide. That suggests that the glide is more graceful and slower. A gentle movement of a hand from the forehead to a pointing position in which the arm is extended to one side is a glide. Romeo speaking beneath the Capulet's balcony "What light from yonder window breaks" would probably use a gliding gesture, but later in his duel with Tybalt he would use both the slash and the thrust. Dancers and skaters glide. Graceful women also glide. Clearly, the glide is a gesture of grace.

The flick is another basic gesture. A quick toss of a coin or a flick of the finger, a hand of an impertinent little minx, or the flap of a foot in a backward kick would all be examples of the flick. Business with fans provides excellent opportunity for the use of the flick; so does the disposal of a cigarette ash or the quick discarding of a touch of lint on a costume. The flick is a fishtail kind of gesture, or the kind of gesture a saucy parakeet might make. It is a gesture especially suitable in comedy and in the establishment of a foppish or flighty character.

Next let us consider the rub. Chin strokers use the rub; so do hand rubbers. A scratch is a rub, so is a shuffle. The brushing of clothes, the polishing of furniture, or the smoothing down of hair are all gestures that employ the rub.

There are two more basic gestures. They are descension and ascension, or the fall and the lift. They are both sufficiently self-explanatory to be disposed of succinctly. Any downward action is a descension. This might be the bowing of the head, the slumping of the shoulders, the lowering of an arm, the slumping of the body, or going from a standing to a sitting position. In contrast, rising from a sitting position to a standing position, lifting an arm or a hand, pulling the body into an erect position, or lifting the head all constitute ascension gestures. All such gestures give the body a lift and therefore symbolize a lift in spirit or thought. All the basic gestures are related to visual dynamics, but the lift and the fall are most readily identified with the strong and weak aspects of kinetics and, like the other aspects of visual dynamics, are part of the ebb and flow of a presentation.

Another important phase of kinetics is the element of timing. It is one thing to know which action best suits the word or phrase or sentence, and something else again to know precisely when to execute the action. Here again, tradition and long practice in the art of oral expression have given us a few reliable rules. Like most rules, they are not infallible; and like most rules, they may at times be broken. However, we should pay some heed to the old adage that only he who has mastered a rule is in a position to break it wisely.

The rules regarding timing are these: first, let us understand that whatever takes place last is the thing that gets the emphasis. When action follows the word or the phrase, action is the important thing. When action precedes the word or phrase, the word or phrase receives the emphasis. When the action accompanies the word or phrase, both receive equal emphasis, and neither is predominant.

In the reading of humorous material, timing takes on a special importance. Here timing must be particularly precise. Whatever action is used must be selected with good judgment and should be thoroughly rehearsed. It is a great mistake to imagine that humor can be brought off successfully by spontaneity alone. Comedy must seem to be spontaneous, but it will seem so only when it is carefully timed and well prepared. Only the amateur fancies he can perform without adequate rehearsing.

Let us remember, too, that reversals are usually surefire in comedy. A strong line followed by a weak movement, or a weak line followed by a strong movement is a sound comedy rule. Also, in comedy the gesture should usually follow the punch line, rather than precede or accompany it.

Timing also involves the handling of the laughs. Since

the object of humor is to provoke laughter from the audience, it is important to know just what to do about that laughter. To the reader of humor, such laughter is the sweetest music this side of heaven, so he must learn to wait for it. However, when the laughter is slow in coming, as it often may be, the reader cannot merely stand waiting for it with a puzzled look of expectation on his face. Instead, he must cover the pause with some appropriate business or facial expression—an expression which is in keeping with the nature of the humor. In that case, if the expected laughter does not come, he is not left with egg on his face, but can proceed with no noticeable interruption in the flow of the performance.

Timing the laugh in terms of its duration is another point demanding comment. A reader who does not know how to break in on a laugh, and lets it run its natural course, will find the tempo of his performance suffering seriously. Furthermore, the audience is likely to laugh itself out before the performance is half over. The trick is to cut in on the laugh before it is quite over and continue with the reading. The rule is to catch the laugh when it is just over its crest. The timing of a laugh is a little like surfing. The reader has to know when to take the wave and when to break from it.

With timing, the basic gestures, and visual dynamics now behind us, we are ready to devote some time to physical preparation. Theory is of value only when we are prepared to use it. Certainly the understanding of theory is part of preparation, but we can put theory into practice only when we are properly prepared physically. This calls for a sensitive awareness of one's physical potentials and for development of those potentials through practice.

The fact that everyone has his own individual physical potentials calls for a good session in front of a mirror on the part of each student. Here let us speak directly to the student. In a shift to second person, we say to you, "Take a long look at yourself in the looking glass. Study your face, your shoulders, your arms, your hands, your whole body. You are looking at what your audience will see when you appear before it. Quite naturally you want the person that audience sees to appear at his best. You want to look well as well as sound well."

Begin with a study of your eyes. Blink, squint, open wide, and see how many moods you can express with your eyes alone. Generally speaking, the eyes are the main focal point of the audience. People will be watching your eyes most of the time, more than any other part of your anatomy. Your eyes must talk quite as actively as your tongue.

While we are on the subject of eyes, let us give some attention to your general focus in terms of the audience. When should you make direct eye contact with your viewers and when should you avoid direct contact? The nature of your presentation gives you the answer. If your performance is presentational you will want to have a great deal of eye contact with your audience. If it is representational you will want none at all. In a presentational performance you are reading directly to the audience, much as though you were making an informal speech or telling a story. If the performance is representational, you are reenacting your story dramatically and must create the illusion of remoteness. This you do by looking over the heads of the audience and never, under any circumstances, into the faces of your spectators.

Extend the study of your eyes to include the forehead, your eyebrows, and the muscles around your eyes. Take note of the many different things you can do with your eyebrows and the variety of expressions that can be achieved with the wrinkles in the forehead. Your wrinkles may be few or virtually nonexistent, but you can frown and you can lift the muscles in your forehead in surprise. The vertical lines of the frown and the horizontal lines of the lift of surprise contribute to your facial mobility.

If you are among those blessed with a mobile face, Fortuna favors you. Make the most of it. If you are like the majority of young students, you may have to overcome the nemesis of an immobile face. You can do this, but you will have to work at it.

Usually the most mobile part of the face is the mouth. Let us focus now on the mouth. Portrait painters generally agree that it is the most difficult part of the face to paint. This may be because it is capable of assuming so many different attitudes.

Study your mouth objectively. What kind of a mouth is it basically? Is it friendly or foreboding, kindly or cruel, cheerful, or gloomy? No one cares to admit that he has a mouth that suggests cruelty or gloominess, but study yours carefully and honestly. When you have satisfied yourself as to the kind of a mouth you have, start experimenting with it. You cannot change the mouth nature has given you, but you can do a lot to alter its range of expression. If the corners turn down excessively, you can compensate by smiling more often. If your mouth is basically petulant, practice looking pleased. If your lips are generally too tight, practice pressing them into a full, generous expression.

Next, work with the cheeks, the jaws, the chin, and even the nose. You may find that the muscles in those parts of your face are altogether too inflexible. You need not be surprised at this, but you should be concerned, concerned enough to practice making faces, all sorts of faces. Making faces in the mirror may seem like a reversion to child's play, but to anyone eager to make his face more expressive it is a necessary procedure.

Isn't this purely mechanical approach highly superficial? Is that the question you were about to ask? It is a natural question and a usual one. Certainly anyone who has heard about the Stanislavski system of acting might legitimately ask such a question. Yes, it is superficial unless we add something. That something is feeling, or, to use Stanislavski's term, inner motivation. Certainly the inner motivation is of the greatest importance. However, all the inner motivation, all the honest feeling, all the sincerity of emotion, all these are of little value if they cannot be effectively expressed, and they certainly cannot be expressed by a face that is too stiff, too immobile, too totally rigid to react to whatever is being felt.

A pianist may feel all the emotions of a Beethoven sonata, but if he doesn't have the fingering technique to express those feelings his emotions merely add up to frustration. An actor may feel fear or anger, but if he can't make his face and body show what he is feeling he isn't much of an actor. An artist needs inner technique, that is, the ability to trigger diverse emotions, but he must have external technique, that is, the mechanics of expression, or all the inner technique in the world will avail him naught. Obviously, what is called for is a balance of internal and external techniques, and this, incidentally, is precisely what Stanislavski required of his actors.

We should keep this balance in mind as we turn now to a consideration of the use of the hands. Study, now, your hands. Regard them as you have never regarded them before. Are your fingers relatively even at the ends, or is your second finger extra long and your fifth finger unusually short? If the former, you probably have excellent finger dexterity. If the latter, you no doubt have trouble coordinating the use of your fingers. Are your hands squarish, or long and tapering? Regardless of their size and shape, they are your hands and must be trained to serve you to the best advantage.

In the interest of such service, open and close them, clench your fists and stretch them out with palms wide open. Hold them out with palms up. Turn them over with palms down. Now do all this looking at them in the mirror. You will soon discover that your hands can speak a language of their own. Hands curved suggest invitation or an indication to follow. Palms held high and turned down suggest benediction, or when turned up, supplication. A forefinger to the lips in any language indicates silence, or "mum's the word."

Consider Shakespeare's reference to hands and lips in the sonnet sequence in *Romeo and Juliet:*

ROMEO   If I profane with my unworthiest hand
            This holy shrine, the gentle fine is this:
            My lips, two blushing pilgrims, ready stand
            To smooth that rough touch with a tender kiss.

JULIET   Good pilgrim, you do wrong your hand too much,
            Which mannerly devotion shows in this;
            For saints have hands that pilgrims' hands do touch,
            And palm to palm is holy palmers' kiss.

ROMEO   Have not saints lips, and holy palmers too?

JULIET   Ay, pilgrim, lips that they must use in prayer.

ROMEO   O, then, dear saint, let lips do what hands do;
            They pray, grant thou, lest faith turn to despair.

JULIET   Saints do not move, though grant for prayers' sake.

ROMEO	Then move not, while my prayer's effect I take.
	Thus from my lips, by yours, my sin is purged.
JULIET	Then have my lips the sin that they have took.
ROMEO	Sin from my lips? O trespass sweetly urged! Give me my sin again.
JULIET	You kiss by the book.

Act I, Scene 5

It should not take more than a few minutes in front of the mirror with your hands in action to cause you to become thoroughly intrigued with the things you can do with your hands. A little experimentation will open a whole new world of possibilities. Never again should you be caught asking that amateurish question, "What should I do with my hands?" Use them. That is the obvious answer. Use them to say what your tongue and face are saying, but use them with discrimination and restraint. An excessive use of hands is as bad or worse than no use at all.

As you study your hands, you will be aware that they are attached to your arms, an obvious observation that has more relevance than might be imagined. Add to this the equally obvious realization that your arms are attached to your shoulders, and the relevance may begin to come clear. Arm movement should be controlled from the shoulders which are in turn controlled from the muscles in the back. Hence the impetus for gestures comes from the back muscles. Conceivably there might be confined hand movement that would be limited to an impetus from the elbows and forearms, but generally speaking gesture impetus should come from the back muscles. Experimentation before the mirror will make this matter apparent.

Look next at your knees. Are they locked in a rigid position, or are they slightly bent and relaxed? If the former, you will give the appearance of a kind of rigid ramrod which is perilously poised for a fall. If the latter, you will appear at ease, yet ready for any movement that may be called for. Locked knees are common among inexperienced performers, so take a good look at your knees and practice moving about and standing with your knees bent slightly in a natural, comfortable position.

Finally, study your feet. The position of your feet is basic to your total stance, so a lot of practice in footwork is in order. It may prove helpful if you begin by deliberately placing your feet in awkward positions such as pointing your toes straight out toward the audience, or turning them in in a pigeon-toed manner. Very soon you will discover that the most comfortable position is the one most graceful and natural. Toes are turned out slightly and the heels are from a few inches to a foot apart with one foot slightly in advance of the other. The weight should be evenly distributed on the balls of both feet and never on the heels. This does not mean that the weight cannot shift from one foot to another and that the basic stance cannot change. On the contrary, the feet should be freely maneuverable, and readily responsive.

Your work before the mirror is not finished with the feet. You should practice various kinds of walks such as the shuffle, the hobble, the stride, the Grecian tread (one foot directly in front of the other), and various other walks that you will hit upon as you experiment. You should practice the various body positions and engage in all kinds of normal and unusual movements. You should try to free yourself of inhibitions and have an unrestrained, carefree time making faces and going through contortions for the sheer delight of developing facial and body freedom. As you develop freedom, you will also be developing discipline. That is the curious dichotomy which is the reward of working before a mirror.

Students who are limited to the internal-technique orientation often look with disdain on those who use the looking glass as a tool of training. There would be justice in their disdain if training were limited to time in front of a mirror, but such should never be the case. In fact, all that we have just been saying is preliminary to the development of inner technique.

However, before we turn to the internal aspect of oral interpretation, there are a few final points that should be made about the visual aspect. The first concerns the quantity of kinetics that should be employed in oral interpretation. This brings us back to a basic controversy. How much of all that we have been discussing is applicable to a public reading? How much is relevant only to acting, and how much may be used in oral interpretation?

Conceivably all of it might be used in oral interpretation at one time or another. Again we stress the fact that oral interpretation can include a great deal of histrionics, but just how much depends upon the nature of the material that is being read and the kind of talent that is doing the reading. Any text that is basically dramatic, or that lends itself to considerable impersonation, certainly invites all the histrionic skill the reader may have at his command. Whether he confines his performance to a lectern and a limited area, or uses the entire stage, he will need to draw upon such visual techniques as we have been discussing.

On the other hand, if the text is chiefly narrative and offers little or no opportunity for impersonation, the reader may still find that he can enhance his performance by making use of many of the techniques mentioned above. Naturally he will, in that case, use these techniques with discretion and good taste. It would be obvious folly, for example, to run the gamut of gestures and facial expression in a recital of poetry or a reading of a novelette.

The other final point to be made is the reminder that oral communication is more than oral interpretation. There are many phases of oral communication that are quite different from the public performance that is implied in formal readings. All those many items spoken of earlier in this book are a part of the general business of oral reading, and certainly such things as annual reports, minutes of meetings, resolutions, and the like, would hardly demand the range of kinetics we have been discussing. Nevertheless, such readings can be considerably enlivened by some knowledge of visual dynamics, basic gestures, and physical preparation. That fact is our conclusive point, and it is that point that we wish to emphasize because it is the general improvement of all oral reading that is our overall concern.

5

Triggering the Imagination: The Mind and Heart of the Matter

The heart of the art is knowing how much heart to put into the art. The art itself is a matter of mind over imagination. Being an art, oral reading is dependent on discipline. Discipline, however, goes beyond the training of tongue, lungs, face, and body. The reading artist must be in command of his mind, emotions, and that most difficult of all things to define, the imagination.

Toward such discipline there are steps to take, but before we take them let us confront another controversy. How much heart should we put into the art? Some say a lot. Some say none. Some say it is imperative to feel everything. Others insist that reading, like acting, or even more than acting, should be purely objective. Which, if either, extreme is right?

We could dismiss the question by simply stating that neither extreme is right, and go in quest immediately for the golden mean, but there is more to the controversy than can be glibly ignored. There is more to explore and the exploration is in itself a fascinating adventure. The adventure begins with a classification of the various kinds of readers.

There are clearly five kinds of readers. Those five include the casual, the imitative, the technical, the egocentric, and the imaginative. When we have analyzed this classification, we will be well on our way to a sound solution to the controversy.

The casual reader is the untrained amateur who reads mostly for the pleasure he gets out of it. His public appearances as a reader are purely occasional. He relies on whatever native talent he may or may not have and does not bother to develop whatever talent he may have. Any artistry he chances to possess is purely intuitive and totally undisciplined. He may be good, or he may be terrible. He may be good at times, quite brilliant in fact, but his performance will be uneven and undependable. He is almost certain to have great inconsistencies in his diction and interpretative conceptions, and his merit as an entertainer is an unreliable factor. He may be engaging and interesting, but is not likely to be consistently so.

In this description of the casual reader, we are referring to the reader who may make casual or occasional public appearances. However, we should include in this category other persons who may have to read for a group of one kind or another from time to time, but do not read for the entertainment of an audience. Such persons, of course, make no pretense at being public readers, and can therefore be excused for a lack of discipline. Nevertheless, we must emphasize that their reading would be much more effective with the kind of training we are advocating.

Next let us consider the imitative reader. He too may

be good at times, depending upon his ability to imitate and the kind of performers he chooses to imitate. He may also be a person with discipline and training, but he uses whatever training he has to copy rather than to create. He is a copycat. The imitative reader has no originality. Unlike the casual reader, who may force his voice and body due to a lack of technique, the imitative reader may present a program that is well thought out and thoroughly prepared, but it will always be an imitation of some other reader or actor, or it may be a combination of tricks he has gained from observing several performers. Lacking in resourcefulness, he falls back on gestures and line readings he has observed and is likely to be extremely repetitious in his performance. Clearly, he has not learned to trigger his imagination.

Turning to the technical reader, he can best be described as a performer with great objectivity. He is the reader who meticulously works out his vocal and visual details and takes great pride in executing them with precision. He does not lose himself in his performance, but rather is in command of everything he does and says. He may or may not perform with emotional integrity, but he hopes always to convey the right emotions through technical facility. More likely than not, he has felt the intrinsic emotions sometime during his preparation, and, having once experienced those feelings, may try to recapture them during performance, but he will not let his emotions get in the way of a smooth technical performance. Actually the technical reader is more likely than not to be the kind who fights shy of what he thinks might be excessive emotion. He is, after all, the objective performer.

The egocentric reader is, as the term implies, a self-centered individual who cannot shed his individuality even for the sake of impersonation. He is always himself in everything he does. He finds it impossible to adapt his personality to the content, but, instead, attempts to bend the content to his personality. He is like the movie star who is always the same in every role he does. The egocentric reader may be as he is because he simply hasn't the gift of impersonation, or he may be simply a stubborn individualist. In either event, he is fatefully inflexible. All performers need a reasonable amount of approbation, but the egocentric reader must have an abundance of it. He loves being in the limelight. He is the kind of person who is constantly "on." This is not to say he may not be entertaining, but his range of entertainment is limited to the limitations of his self-centered personality.

The most distinctive and usually the most effective of the five kinds of readers is the imaginative reader. He is the one who can trigger his imagination. What that means is that he has enough inner technique to spark whatever emotion is needed, and enough external technique to channel the desired emotion into believable expression. He makes use of emotional memory to recall incidents in his own life that are comparable to the situation called for in the text. He is able to use that recall to create the necessary feeling. If an emotion is beyond his empirical ken, he may draw upon dreams, or resort to an experience that is similar enough to be convincing. He is likely to read with a great deal of emotional integrity, and feel deeply everything he says and does. Usually he is a person with a strong native imagination, but it is an imagination that is readily accessible and is subject to immediate summons by his conscious mind. We might say the imaginative reader has a hot line from his conscious to his subconscious mind.

From these five varied approaches to reading we should

be able to glean a clue toward the settlement of the controversy. We still see that some readers feel deeply and some do not, that some try to put feeling into everything they are saying and doing, and that others treat their actions and line readings with objectivity, in short, that some are emotional and some technical. However, the clue to the solution does not actually lie in that divergence at all. The clue comes from the fact that both the technical reader and the imaginative reader may be effective and convincing. Why? Because the question is not whether or not the reader feels or doesn't feel, but rather whether or not the audience feels or doesn't feel. The reader's objective is to move his audience. He must give his audience an emotional and intellectual experience. What he himself experiences is actually beside the point. He may shed real tears or only pretend to shed real tears, but his audience must experience the emotion that provokes the tears, and must, therefore, be convinced that the reader is likewise experiencing the emotion. In other words, it is not what the reader is feeling, but what the audience believes he is feeling that matters. That is the essence of communication, and that is the solution to the controversy.

How does one acquire the magic for moving an audience? How? Through the power of imagination. It would be more accurate to say, through the expansion and control of imagination. Imagination being one of man's most valuable assets, any hints as to its expansion and control should be arresting to everyone, but especially to all those who perform for the public. Here, then, begins a lesson in living, but it is a lesson directed particularly to the reader who is interested in something other than the sound of his own voice.

He who would move an audience must first wake up his own brain. The average person uses only a fraction of his brain. How do we waken that vast slumbering portion? How do we trip those millions of brain cells deep in the nether world of the subconscious? How do we perk up the pituitary glands? How do we trigger the imagination?

There are ways, but first we must recognize that all the ways are not right for all the people. Again let us do a bit of categorizing. Let us explore four fundamental motivations which seem to furnish the human drive. From these four motivations each student will have to try to discover which one or which combination is right for him.

As preliminary to this quest, let us clarify our goal. Our goal is the maximum expansion of mind and imagination. Our goal is something else as well. It is to establish identity. It is to ask again the inescapable question, the question we are forever trying hopelessly to evade, the question "Who am I?" Who am I in the cosmic scheme of things? Who am I in relation to the world about me, the world beyond me, the human world, the material world, and that unseen world of the spirit? Who am I?

The goal may be sought through four motivations. The first we will call, for want of a better term, the philosophical motivation. Those who are philosophically motivated enjoy the pursuit of knowledge; often it is knowledge for the sake of knowledge. They are intrigued by ideas, abstractions, poetic concepts, and religion or religions.

For the philosophically motivated, the route to a wider horizon of imagination is through reading, meditation, and discussion. They must be encouraged to seek the goal in the way that is right for them. They must be encouraged to spend time alone, to develop their powers of meditation. They should be reminded what Socrates did for the imaginations of the Athenian youths. Like Socrates, they must seek the larger self beneath and beyond the surface self. Like Socrates, they must learn to listen, learn to ask, learn to reflect. As he listens, asks, and reflects, a philosophically motivated person cannot help expanding his imagination.

One thing the philosophically motivated person is likely to possess or can easily acquire is perspective. He is able to think of himself in the third person, is able to stand off and have a look at himself. Anyone who develops this ability is not likely to take himself over-seriously and therefore will maintain his sense of humor. Perspective is an excellent thing for a reader. It is also an ideal vantage for imagination expansion.

The second impetus to motivation we should like to discuss is love. "Love," that badly abused, grossly misused four-letter word can be a magic key to imagination. While it is true that everyone is motivated by love, or the inversion of love, hate, it is equally true that some are more love oriented and more love motivated than others. We do not all have the same capacity for love, and we do not all share the same concept of the word. An expansion of concept can lead to an expansion of capacity, as we shall soon discover.

We begin with love of self. We must begin there, because no man can get far with the "love thy neighbor as thyself" idea until he learns to love himself. Indeed, the degree with which we are capable of comprehending that commandment is based upon the degree of self-love. What is self-love? Isn't self-love the very thing most decent people are trying to overcome? Isn't it the essence of conceit, the basis for egotistic self-centeredness, and utter selfishness?

The first step toward understanding self-love is to knock that concept into a cocked hat. Real self-love is none of those things. On the other hand, self-love is the basis for self-respect, self-esteem, self-confidence, and self-reliance. It is a recognition of self as a marvel of creation, a singular extension of the infinite manifested in the finite. It is a full and wholesome acceptance of oneself for what one is. Limitations, blemishes, personality twirks, handicaps, a face that only a mother could love, are all accepted along with whatever virtues, talents, and marks of beauty one may have. Self-love is, in fact, a first step toward self-identity.

The next step in self-identity is also the next step in love. One identifies himself in relation to another person. Baby John is the manchild of his mother Mary. A child's first extension of love is toward those who give him security and respond to his wants. This is the love of the dependent for those on whom he depends. That kind of love is not limited to the child-parent relationship. It is often in evidence in the boss-employee relationship, the old master-servant combination, and is often found among siblings and among friends.

Paralleling the dependent love is the parental love, or the love one has for those who are dependent upon him. Examples of this kind of love have their obvious examples in an inversion of the sequence mentioned above. Yet beyond the parent-for-child, employer-for-employee example, we find this love for those who need us reaching far beyond the home, the neighborhood, and the nation. It is this love for those who need us that is the basis for most of our charities and much of our legislation.

Admittedly the love for status and prestige is sometimes behind our gifts to charities, but that, like the love for fortune, fame, and power is a distorted kind of love, a love for false gods, and, though it may be a stimulus to the imagination, deserves short shrift in our major discussion. Not the false gods, but the manifold, positive manifestation of love is our major concern.

Dare we introduce in the major concern the dynamite

of romantic love? We dare. It must be introduced even though an introduction is about all our sketchy treatment can be called. However, romantic love needs no introduction. It will be no stranger to those who read this book. Furthermore, all who read will be well aware that a subject which has been a prime source of books and plays for centuries can hardly be exhausted in a paragraph or two. Therefore we need do little more than acknowledge it.

It should be borne in mind that children are not the only things romantic love begets. It begets family love, that old time-honored love of kin for kin, that primal love of clan. Out of the love of clan we find another stick of dynamite. It is the love of race for race. Presto comes the clash of integration versus segregation, and we have another explosion.

The ramifications of that explosion furnish material enough to stretch the imagination aplenty, and the old, old conflict of love against hate bangs at the door.

Akin to love of clan and race is love of country. Again the danger flag goes up! Patriotism, or chauvinism? When does the former become the latter? How patriotic can we afford to be without becoming too nationalistic? How nationalistic can we afford to be and still love all mankind? Should we love all mankind? Should we at least try to love all mankind? What do the rules we live by tell us? What does the conscience say? These questions, calculated to whet the imagination, may be abetted by the following quotations:

> One who would guide a leader of men in the uses of life will warn him against the use of arms for conquest.
> Lao-tse

> Oppressive rule is more cruel than a tiger.
> Confucius

Only those are worthy to govern who would rather be excused.
Ibid.

He who exercises government by means of his virtue may be compared to the north polar star which keeps its place and all the stars turn toward it.
Ibid.

To govern is to keep straight.
Ibid.

What need is there of the death penalty in government? If you showed a sincere desire to be good, your people would likewise be good.
Ibid.

The virtue of the prince is like unto wind; that of the people like unto grass, for it is the nature of grass to bend when the wind blows upon it.
Ibid.

Poverty is the parent of revolution and crime.
Aristotle, *Politics,* Book II

That judges of important causes should hold office for life is not a good thing, for the mind grows old as well as the body.
Ibid.

If liberty and equality, as is thought by some, are chiefly to be found in democracy, they will be at best attained when all persons alike share in the government to the utmost.
Ibid., Book IV

The best political community is formed by citizens of the middle class.
Ibid.

Inferiors revolt in order that they may be equal, and equals that they may be superior. Such is the state of mind which creates revolutions.
Ibid., Book V

Revolutions break out when opposite parties, the rich and the poor, are equally balanced, and there is little or nothing between them.
Ibid.

The men that stood for office, noted for acknowledged worth,
And for manly deeds of honour, and for honourable birth;
Train'd in exercise and art, in sacred dances and in song,
All are ousted and supplanted by a base ignoble throng.
Aristophanes, *The Frogs*

If we withdraw the confidence we placed
In these our present statesmen, and transfer it
To those whom we mistrusted heretofore,
This seems I think our fairest chance for safety:
If with our present counsellors we fail,
Then with their opposites we might succeed.
Ibid.

A lively and lasting sense of filial duty is more effectually impressed on the mind of a son or daughter by reading King Lear, than by all the dry volumes of ethics, and divinity, that ever were written.
Thomas Jefferson

The God who gave us life, gave us liberty at the same time.
Ibid.

Error of opinion may be tolerated where reason is left free to combat it.
Ibid.

When a man assumes a public trust, he should consider himself as public property.
Ibid.

Indeed, I tremble for my country when I reflect that God is just.
Ibid.

What we obtain too cheap, we esteem too lightly; it is dearness only that gives everything its value.
Thomas Paine

War involves in its progress such a train of unforeseen and unsupposed circumstances that no human wisdom can calculate the end. It has but one thing certain, and that is to increase taxes.
Ibid.

> The world is my country,
> All mankind are my brethren,
> To do good is my religion,
> I believe in one God and no more.
> *Ibid.*

The sublime and the ridiculous are often so nearly related, that it is difficult to class them separately.
Ibid.

The Greeks had a word the early Christians liked. They liked it enough to try to live by it. It was the word *agape*. It means "brotherly love." For a long while it was thought that *agape* was the highest kind of love, the ultimate ideal toward which all men should strive. However, of late another word in the language of love is receiving increasing attention. It is the Buddhist word *karuna,* meaning universal compassion. Here is a seismic love significant enough to shake the earth, or, if not the earth, at least all the creatures on it. Here is a love, in fact, that is no longer earthbound, but reaches spaceward to embrace the stars, the galaxies, and the very cosmos.

It may be that we are on the brink of revelation. It may be that all we have known before is blind ignorance in the face of this potential comprehension. It may be that love holds many mysteries yet to be revealed. Who knows but what the era of revelation may have been ushered in when those pioneering astronauts, all men of faith, of love, of gentle yet courageous good will, called to the earth from their orbiting of the moon and prayed that now-famed Christmas message: "In the beginning God created the heavens and the earth."

Another fundamental motivator is work. To those who are work motivated, it may come as something of a surprise to learn that not everyone is motivated by this fine old Calvinistic virtue. To those who are work motivated, work is a virtuous attribute. To those who are not so motivated it is often looked upon as a curse. Which is it, a virtue or a curse? Let us examine work in terms of what it may do to stimulate imagination.

Whether work is physical or intellectual, it is a means of self-expression and a venture toward self-fulfillment. It is a means by which one seeks to justify one's existence, to balance the ledger of life, and to give something in exchange for the gift of life. There are people who are lazy for one reason or another, and those who are born loafers, but most people want to feel useful and they can usually do this best when they feel they are doing something useful. To most people, the need to feel needed is congenital.

At the heart of this need is the crux of the work motivation. It is a sense of responsibility. One likes to feel responsible for something, to feel that he alone can do a particular job. The old adage, "Let George do it," is not for the work-motivated person. George would be sure to foul things up, or, if he didn't, he would be doing a job intended for someone else. George might take over in case of illness, but a conscientious person wants to work when he is well, whatever the job may be.

The job may be a study assignment, or a part in a play, or a reading commitment. It may be simple or complex, part time or full time, strenuous or relaxing, but whatever it is, it is something to be done, and doing it is the all-important thing. To the people who are work motivated, idleness is a miserable state. Without work of some sort they are restless and often ill-tempered. With no responsibility, they feel inferior, impatient, and morose. Everyone knows the troubles that result from excessive unemployment.

To be sure, there are those who would rather collect unemployment insurance than hold a steady job, and those who would rather loaf on a welfare allotment than work for a paycheck, but they are decidedly not among the work-motivated citizens of our land. By the very nature of their contrast they give accent to the next point we want to make. That point has to do with remuneration. Nobody likes to work for nothing, and the laborer is worthy of his hire, but to the work-motivated man or woman the pay is not the only incentive. It may be the chief incentive for work that is sheer drudgery, or on jobs that are dull and boring, but it is rarely the only incentive. Anyone trapped in monotonous, backbreaking work would be glad to find another job, but that does not mean that he does not want to work.

In order further to elucidate work as a motivating force, we must distinguish between work and toil. Certainly to slave away at a job that is sheer drudgery or pure monotony is far from an ideal way to stimulate the imagination. People who are predominantly motivated by a compulsion to work are not necessarily the toilers. On the contrary, they are the people who like to keep busy. They must be engaged in some activity, either physical or intellectual, in order to maintain an emotional equilibrium. They invent things to do in order to avoid idleness. To them, even leisure time cannot be idle time.

Leisure in an affluent, technological society is a proliferating luxury. It is also a prodigious problem for those who are not capable of using it imaginatively. Work motivated individuals do not think of leisure as an antonym to work, but rather as an opportunity to engage in a chosen work. We find proof of this in the millions of retired people who are working harder than they ever worked before at hobbies, charities, or new careers. Often it is voluntary work that does most toward widening the horizons of the imagination. The volunteer and the person who is out to make the most of his leisure are usually doing what they want to do for the sheer joy of doing it. In that frame of mind they are likely to be more inventive and more open to the free flow of ideas.

The worker, voluntary or otherwise, seeks to fulfill the human need for self-respect and self-reliance. Through the dignity of work he strives to complete what nature began in him in infancy. Through the motivation of work he finds, or seeks to find, his reason for being, and, in pursuit of that discovery, he plumbs the pits of his imagination.

The fourth and final fundamental motivation is scientific. Here, open wide the gates! For the scientifically motivated individual, the gates open not merely to a cloister where he might meditate, or to a garden where he might taste the fruits of love, or to a city of industry. Instead, they open to a continent, a galaxy, a universe. The gates open, and a superbomb of scientific and technological knowledge explodes in our faces.

Being empirically oriented, the person who is scientifically motivated will seek to widen his imagination through experiment. It is his nature to experiment. He will experiment even though the price of experimentation is sometimes too high to pay. Such is the case when shortcuts to imagination are sought by means of certain well-known psychedelic drugs. Drugs may one day waken the imagination, but thus far they only create illusions and hallucinations and, in many cases, irretrievable harm, both mental and physical.

More than all others, the scientist knows that the way to the imagination is through clear-headed thinking and not through a pill or a shot in the arm. Clear-headed, disciplined thinking, matching fact to fact, testing this and that, learning by proof, and double proof of proof—such is the method of the one who is scientifically motivated.

Actually, the programming of new experiments can in itself become a horrendous exercise of the imagination. "If this is done, would this result? If such and such were tried, what would result?" What can be used that has been researched? What new research is needed? What soft ware should be fed into the computer? The imagination is not only exercised, it is staggered.

No doubt discussion of the scientific motivation need

not be prolonged. Those who have it are certain to have access to a plethora of stimulating material. Those who are not so motivated are probably already somewhat dismayed by the proliferation of scientific and technological knowledge.

Our choice of four fundamental motivations is obviously far from comprehensive. Naturally there are many other kinds of motivations. However, upon careful examination it will likely be discovered that most of them can correlate conveniently with these four. In any event, our object has been to open pathways to the imagination, not to delve into a depth study of motivation. The object of this discussion has been to expand the imagination, to enlarge the capacity of the imagination of the reader, and to give him greater depths from which to draw when he tries to trigger his imagination.

With the recognition of the various kinds of readers and the discussion of the fundamental motivations, we can conclude this chapter. However, in conclusion, we must emphasize again the value and importance of the application of all this to oral reading of any kind. No one will want to make a dramatic production of something like the reading of a resolution, or an announcement of a coming event, but the astute and alert student will be aware of how the overtones of this background can be applied to virtually every kind of public reading. The application to oral reading as an art form is, of course, readily apparent, but this text is not for the public reader alone. It is meant to be helpful to all those who are faced with the necessity of reading something aloud, either often or occasionally. Such reading will be impressively more effective when the imagination is tapped and the full force of mind and emotion are focused on the project.

6

Corporate Reading: Choric Drama, Verse Choir, and Readers' Theatre

All through this text thus far we have dealt with the reader as a soloist. Now it is time to think of him as a member of an ensemble. That he will appear as a soloist in many public readings is advocated, hoped for, and predicted, but his potential participation in the various phases of corporate reading is a matter we must not neglect. This is a contingent of oral interpretation that has values of great significance, values which are all too often totally neglected.

Aside from the artistic and literary rewards one may expect from corporate reading, there are significant therapeutic values to be considered. Corporate reading can be a veritable group-therapy experience. Yet it is, or at least should be, a type of group therapy that is free from the therapeutic atmosphere of the clinic.

This is not to find fault with clinics, or with the clinical method of group therapy. Rather, it is merely a recognition of the fact that students can often be helped more directly when they are in situations in which there is no mention of, and certainly no emphasis on, therapy. Students who are simply trying to do their best in a group assignment are likely to feel much more free than when they are in situations in which they may feel they are under special surveillance. Their focus is on performance rather than on what someone is going to think of them each time they speak.

Examples are legion. Jane was a recluse, shy, withdrawn, with a voice to match her timorous personality. She was given a role in a choric drama. Nobody said anything to her about her shyness, but she was directed to project and play her role with feeling the same as everyone else. She struggled at first, but in a short while she found her voice and found great satisfaction in playing her part with genuine emotion.

Another example was Timmy, who hated poetry. He not only hated poetry, he hated everything about the class and the course, including the teacher. He was a rebel looking for a cause. He found the cause most unexpectedly one day in a most unexpected place. He found the cause in one of Dylan Thomas's poems. Suddenly he found he could identify with Thomas. Nobody, least of all the teacher, had paid much attention to his rebellious spirit, but he did get marked attention when his voice came booming through in a verse-choir reading of the poem. His voice was good and his comprehension of the verse was keen and he was praised both by teacher and by classmates. Approbation being a thing he had had little of until then, it was pure champagne to him, and he got better and better each time the poem was rehearsed. Did he reform utterly and suddenly become a nice guy completely rid of his negativism? No, not completely. But he did find something he could take hold of and his attitude continued to improve.

Then there was Mike, a cocky, overly self-confident and thoroughly obnoxious young man who rubbed everyone the wrong way. He seemed to have talent, but both it and he were totally undisciplined. It was obvious to some that his cockiness was a cover for his lack of discipline, so he was wisely cast in a role in a Readers' Theatre production that called for considerable discipline. It happened to be a role he was eating his heart out for, but he was told that he had the part on a trial basis. He would be allowed to play it only if he came through satisfactorily at the first read-through. An amazing humility possessed young Mike, and his reading at the first rehearsal was a surprise to everyone. All the cockiness was gone. He read with careful concentration, and it was obvious that he had studied the part seriously. He was commended and given criticisms along with all the others in the cast, and the next time through he was even better. In the study of that role Mike discovered discipline and he was well on his way to whipping his personal problem.

One more example should be cited because it was an extreme case. There was a girl—we'll call her Sally. Sally, it was learned, came from a home where there was little or no affection, certainly never any demonstration of affection. There was something in her background that is still a mystery. All we knew was that the girl couldn't talk. She would smile, sweetly, and shake her head, but say nothing. When called on in class, she would turn beet red and completely clam up. We knew from the few words she had managed to get out during private conversation that there was nothing organically wrong. Her speech mechanism was normal, but she had some sort of a psychological block. Yet she could read with a group. Read with a group she did, over and over, until the time came for her to solo. On the first try she didn't make it. Nobody jumped on her, nobody scolded. Her turn came around again. Still silence, but this time a long silence. Her cue was read again. Another long silence.

"We can't go on until we hear your line," the teacher said quite casually. Another try, another silence. "We'll wait until you can read your line," said the teacher. They waited and waited, and finally Sally spoke her line, almost inaudibly, but she spoke it. The next time through she spoke it again, this time with a little more confidence. So it went on, with Sally gradually improving. Then came her chance to play a role, a real role in a real play. Rehearsals were pure agony for her, yet she loved the theatre and wanted to act more than anything she could think of. She managed to get up in the role and played it with a considerable degree of success. All the while she was emerging from her cocoon more and more and soon reached the place where she would respond to comments from her fellow students. Eventually she reached the place where she was initiating conversation. Her progress continued until she was almost entirely over her shyness. We say almost, because she will probably never be exactly aggressive, but she overcame her basic problem, and it was working with the group that did it.

Therapy aside, though it should never be purely an aside, let us delve into choric drama, verse choir, and readers' theatre. These are the major aspects of corporate reading. Other than therapy, which is certainly not the main aim of corporate reading, what are the reasons for including it in a normal communications program? This is a question that must be answered sensibly if we are to justify the inclusion of this chapter in this text. If there is nothing special about corporate reading, nothing that hasn't already been covered, why bother with a discussion of the subject? There is something special about it. It is to the student of speech and drama, and for the student of literature, what the orchestra, the choir, the band, a combo, or a chamber group is to the music student. To the public it offers a distinctive art form.

Thus far in this text we have treated reading as a solo activity, and, as such, it has values which have been established both implicitly and explicitly. However, to neglect the concert values of reading would be to sell the student short. In fact, many students may gain far more from corporate reading than from the more conventional aspect of the subject.

In corporate reading the student learns team work. In solo reading he does not. Yet team work is an essential part of everyone's training for life. Most of what we do today in industry, business, education, the professions, and the arts we do in concert with others. Important as individualism is, and much as we need to protect it, we live in a cooperative society and are increasingly interdependent on one another.

In corporate reading the individual is responsible to the group. He is no longer the soloist or the star, the one-man show. He is a vital part of a unit. As a member of an ensemble he has new obligations and new opportunities. Let us consider his obligations.

As a member of a cast or a group-reading project he must meet whatever rehearsal schedule is required. He must be at rehearsals on time and prepared to invest his time intelligently and industriously. If he is late, he cheats the others as well as himself out of rehearsal time, time which will have to be made up later, often at his inconvenience quite as much as the inconvenience of the others.

If he fails to appear for a rehearsal, he throws the whole project off schedule, and may cause an extra rehearsal to be added to the schedule. However, in meeting rehearsals, he is adding immeasurably to his maturity as he develops dependability.

While in rehearsal, the student is fulfilling other obligations. He is, or should be, picking up his cues with alacrity and giving cues clearly and accurately. He is listening to his colleagues and responding with meaningful readings and with a voice that blends with the others. He is taking directions and learning to execute them with dispatch. He is learning to take criticisms and sharpening his own critical faculties. As he gains confidence in himself he is contributing to the confidence of his fellow-performers.

This matter of confidence has special significance. In corporate reading students develop a trust in themselves and in one another. Each has to come in on cue, to give the other the support he needs, to respond, to react, to build the scene, in short to work as a team, and until he can develop trust in others he is likely to be a lonely, fearful individual. Very soon the student discovers that any trust implies a gamble, but he also learns that it is better to gamble in that way and lose occasionally than to be a perpetual doubter. Doubt and uncertainty in corporate reading are hazards to the art and blocks in the way of personal development.

Out of mutual trust comes group spirit. That spirit is enhanced by the corporate desire to excel. There is no room for temperamental stars in corporate reading, be it choric drama, verse choir, or readers' theatre. Each person wants not only to do his best but also for his cohorts to do their best, because he knows their best will make his best look better and vice versa.

As is implied in the paragraphs above, obligations are interwoven with opportunities. That is, of course, as it should be. The fusion of opportunity with obligation is a feature of corporate reading. It may be apparent in ordinary oral reading, but it is always heightened in a group effort.

As we turn to a detailed discussion of the three groupings under corporate reading, let us first explain that our grouping is somewhat arbitrary. Other forms of corporate reading might be included, such as chamber theatre, reading rehearsals, poetry ensembles, but the techniques we shall discuss apply quite generally to all corporate reading. However, we do need to make a distinction between choric drama, verse choir, and readers' theatre.

Strictly speaking the term *choric drama* applies to a type of play in which a speaking chorus is predominant. For example, in the choric drama *World Without End*, which has been performed extensively throughout the English-speaking world, the various members of the chorus play all the roles, some appearing in diverse roles. However, in the choric passages everyone speaks and moves as a member of the chorus.

In this discussion we extend the term choric drama to include any play in which there is a speaking chorus, such as the Greek tragedies and comedies and T. S. Eliot's *Murder in the Cathedral*. Most of the oral techniques used in choric drama are also used in verse choir work. For that reason let us discuss verse choir before articulating the techniques. Any group of any size, banded together to read poetry aloud in concert, could be called a verse choir. During the second quarter of this century the verse-choir movement was quite popular, and there are still several groups that are active. Usually the verse choir is directed and rehearsed, though the director may or may not conduct the choir as it performs.

Both in verse choir and choric drama the performance objectives include precision in rhythm and articulation, vocal orchestration, and projection of meaning and emotional impact. In the achieving of these objectives all the techniques discussed in the earlier chapters of this text may be employed from time to time, but their employment takes on a very interesting application. Let us look at each objective in terms of technique.

When we say rhythmic precision we refer to the various tempi as well as the use of rubato. The tempo of any poem or choric passage from a play is determined by the content and by the director's concept, but each variation in tempo must be firmly set in rehearsal and every member of the chorus must, of course, adhere to the fixed tempo. Any deviation from tempo is disastrous, for the obvious reason that people speaking together must speak together. The same principle holds true of rubato. The phrasing must be precise and in perfect unison.

Precision in diction is also called for with no deviation. Half the chorus cannot be using a reflex *r* when the other half is pronouncing a soft *r,* for instance, and one flat *a* where a broad *a* is called for would be a verbal sore thumb. The articulation must be equally precise. Attacks and releases, the sustaining of vowels, and the sounding of final consonants have to be as carefully worked out as they are in a singing choir. In fact, some such scoring as is suggested in chapter 3 is an excellent technique. The precision carries through, of course, in the use of all the other elements, most particularly pause and stress. Pitch, like tempo, is established in rehearsal, as are the various dynamic levels. Quality, too, is usually preestablished, but quality enters into the orchestration along with melody.

Orchestrating for a verse choir or a speaking chorus is one of the most fascinating things about the art. To orchestrate with human voices is a challenge for any teacher or director, to say nothing of the students fortunate enough to be involved. Human voices, even when they are not singing voices, have exciting potentials. There is no way to describe accurately on paper what can be done with quality, color, and combination. All we can do is to indicate a few steps that may be taken.

The first step is to recognize that the human voice is a remarkable instrument which, when properly trained and directed, can do amazing things. Add to this the fact that a combination of voices, when imaginatively orchestrated, can create breathtaking effects. They can do more than convey content. They can run the gamut of emotion, create mood, and project the thrust of impact.

In order to orchestrate most effectively, the director must become thoroughly familiar with the overall quality of his speaking chorus and with the unique quality of each individual voice. He may, for example, want to single out certain voices for solo passages, or he may want to combine two or more voices for a particular effect. A high, eerie soprano, for example, might be combined with an earthy bass. A clarion tenor quality might blend with a lush, rich contralto. Familiarity with each individual voice will enable the director to determine its vocal range, as well as its quality and timbre. As the ranges are defined, the choir is divided into high voices, medium voices, and low voices. This provides the basis for a three-tone harmony in contrast to the two-tone effect often produced by verse choirs through a simple division of light and dark voices. Triads are always much more interesting than a dual-pitch combination of voices.

The interval between the high and the medium and the medium and the low voices will determine the nature of the harmony that is to be produced. Generally speaking, the most desirable interval between the voices is a major third, but the interval may and should vary for both aesthetic and dramatic effect. Furthermore, the interval should not be constantly maintained. Many, if not most, passages may be most effective when read in unison. It is that shift from harmony to unison and back again that gives the quality of uniqueness to a verse-speaking chorus.

The element of melody is endemic to the orchestration. Through many readings and much rehearsing the chorus will find the melody that best conveys the meaning. Once the most meaningful melody or line is discovered, it should be fixed as the accepted melody. In choric reading a consensus melody is discovered and established. This is not necessarily an arbitrary choice by the director. Rather it is a reading that the group itself discovers. Once discovered, it becomes the authentic melody from which there should be no deviation.

There should be no deviation because the power of the line is dependent upon the unanimity of its delivery. A line delivered in three or four different melodies would result in nothing but confusion on the part of the audience. Let us quickly add that what is true of melody is likewise true of the elements of rubato, pause, and stress.

Now let us quickly add that these melodic patterns may be duplicated in various pitches. Enter harmony! This is where the high, medium, and low voices enter into the total sound. Each voice group maintains its own pitch range independently of the others, and the end result is a basic melody presented in three different pitch levels, producing a harmonic effect that can be, when well done, literally spine tingling.

Having said thus much about the merits of harmony in choric reading, let us hasten to admit that all need not be harmonious. Depending on the content—we are always dependent upon content—a dissonant effect may be much more impressive. Often the content may call for cacophony. The jangle of voices may often be much more expressive of the meaning. However, even a jangle must be well disciplined. In choric reading, nothing can be left to chance. All effects must be intricately worked out and well rehearsed.

Is there, then, no place for spontaneity in choric reading? There is, but the spontaneity must be expressed through the emotions rather than through the rhetoric. The concert master in a symphony orchestra may play spontaneously, but he must play within the structure of the symphony, within his relative relation to the other instruments, and within the beat of the conductor. Thus it is with a member of a speaking chorus. He is, by the very nature of the medium, restricted. But within the range of that restriction he is at liberty to be spontaneous.

We offer now some samples of material suitable for choric reading—scenes from plays in which a chorus is featured, and poems particularly suitable for verse choirs.

FULL CHORUS. All breathing life, re-live! Transcend the time, transcend the age. Man can emerge from time, man can emerge from chaos. Man over masses—triumphant, resplendent man, redeem your soul, regain your identity. Rebuild your culture. All breathing men through the mystery of breathing, breathe again; breathe into being a resurrected race. Rise from the crucifixion of civilization, through the crucible of redemption, rise! Re-

live—men and women of the new millennium, re-live, re-live, re-live!
ONE MAN. Out of the West I rise—I rise out of the hemisphere of the West—somewhere I lived before, yet I am he from whom shall spring the new race—
ANOTHER MAN. I am the seed of the Western race—old continents are forgotten, yet I remember the good and ill of other civilizations—I am the seed of the new-born man of the West.
ANOTHER MAN. I am the seed of the man of the West.
ALL MEN. We are the seed of the Western race—we are the new-born race of the West. How long have we slept in the unknown age? Deep in the ancient Aztec dust, far behind the Mayas, men fought their way through space, grappled through time, conquered environment, were conquered by environment—lived, died—They who lived and died are in our thoughts and dreams—They who were dead now live—We are the resurrected; we are the resurrected. We are the men of the new-born West—the resurrected men of the resurrected West.
FULL CHORUS. We are the men and the women of the West—
ALL WOMEN. The sea shines in the new sun.—The sea to the east and the sea to the west—
FULL CHORUS. The continents of the West shine.—The age is new; time begins and the race of men is clean. The end of the age, the dawn of the age; the world is new, the earth is young.—All men are young.—Time is forgotten; endless time.—Faith transcends! Oh, men and women of our time, this is the time, this is the age.

Albert Johnson, *World Without End*,
Baker's Plays, 1937

WOMEN. We have heard the knell of impending doom. We have seen the signs.
The moon, bloodred, the cry of the loon, we have seen, we have heard the signs.
The Allhallows creatures howl in the night and a frost-like chill walks abroad.
We have seen and heard and smelt the signs in the smell of autumn rot.
We have heard the screech owl cry all night and the bats fly low in the wood shade.
We have felt, and smelt, and heard the things, the things that all men fear.
Will it happen tomorrow, today, tonight, and to whom, to whom, to whom?
ONE MAIDEN. My love rode out to the grey, grey sea.
SECOND MAIDEN. My love is a knight of the king.
THIRD MAIDEN. I know my love will come back to me. I know, I hope, I dream.
FIRST MAIDEN. (*Singing through the following*):
If I had a ribbon bow to bind my hair;
If I had a ribbon bow, my love would think me fair.
FIRST MIDDLE-AGED WOMAN. When I knew in my heart I would have a child, I rejoiced like Sarah of old.
SECOND MIDDLE-AGED WOMAN. When my first-born came, the earth was green and the orchard in full bloom.
THIRD MIDDLE-AGED WOMAN. It's a funny thing, I've always thought, how we always forget the pain, but we always do. We remember the pride, remember the joy, and we always forget the pain.
FIRST OLD WOMAN. When they brought him home, my only son, and I saw him still and cold, I wanted to die, I tried to die . . . my son . . . oh why, oh why?

SECOND OLD WOMAN. We never know why, or how, or when. We never know much, not matter how much we learn.
THIRD OLD WOMAN. We never know much, but this much we know: we are born, we beget, and we die, and there must be a reason, a purpose, a plan, even a reason why we know not why.
ALL WOMEN. We have heard the bell, have seen the signs, though we know not the plan, the why, or where.
The oak knows not when the leaf will fall, or the why of the leaf and the falling.
The eagle soars to the hill, to the sun, and suddenly falls without warning.
A man may laugh all night with joy, and lie on his bier tomorrow.
And a man may dance on the top of the world, and the cheering world dance with him.
But he stands alone, a lonely soul, when the angel of death stands near him.
We have felt and seen and smelt the sign. And the sign is here, and the time.

                    Albert Johnson, *Everyman,*
                    from *Church Plays and How*
                    to Stage Them, United Church
                    Press, 1966.

WOMEN. Can the quarry fly from the falcon's eye, from the spaniel's scent, from the sting of the flint?
Can the hunted run from the hunter's hound without running round in a circle?
I have seen a cedar touching a star, tall in the white, white winter.
I have seen that cedar limp in the snow, prey to the woodman's axe.

Oh, the red ripe apples of late September fulfill the April blossoms, and the dead, rotten apples of late December fall back to the earth again.
Who can pull back the tide? Who can stop the moon pull on the impending tide?
In the spring of the year, in the May of the year, the sweet sap flows in the maple, and the May of the year is the time when orioles are mating.
Can you stop the flow of the maple sap, or an egg from incubating?
Can you hold back the night with a candle light?
Can you stop the dawn with a whistle?
FIRST MAIDEN. I gave my love a red, red rose, and my love rode out and away, but my love will bring a ribbon bow to bind my hair in May.
SECOND MAIDEN. My love sailed off on St. Stephen's Day, on a cold gray day in December.
My love will return on Valentine's Day, my love will return and remember.
THIRD MAIDEN. There is death and danger in the winter wars, and the knights of the king are harried.
But the spring of the year is the joy of the year, when my love and I will be married.
THREE MIDDLE-AGED WOMEN. We have heard the gossip in chimney corners, the whispering in pantry, the whispering in church, and tide in, tide out, the talk is the same. Sow wild, reap wild . . . the story's the same. And the reaper comes, come the autumn.
THREE OLD WOMEN. Dreaming by the fire in winter, we remember other times, summertimes, but the summer ends, the August sun goes down, and the long hay-scented day turns to night, a long, long night of winter.
ALL WOMEN. We have known the cycle of seasons, we

have felt the cycle of love, but the cycle of life, the cycle of time is the tune, and the time of the hunter's song to the fearful hoot of the hunter's horn, and the beat of the hoofs of the hunter's horse, and the howl of falcon and hound.

Ibid.

OLD WOMEN. Will the world be different because we came? Will the course be altered, the way changed? Will the sons of our sons be blessed because of the sons we had? Will the times be sad or happy times because of the way we spend our time?
MIDDLE-AGED WOMEN. Shall I take the fork in the road to the right? Shall I take the turn to the left? And who will know, in a thousand years, if the turn I took was right? And who will know today or tonight if the thought I think is dark or bright, or the prayer I pray is for good or ill, or the thing I will is well?
THREE MAIDENS. Will the wild, red rose that sweetens the lane be sweeter in days to come because I kissed my love in the lane where the wild, red roses grow?
ALL WOMEN. We have heard the word of decision.
We have spoken the word, sometimes with thinking, sometimes not thinking.
We have said the thing, or thought the thing, or done the deed that changed the pattern, or planted the seed, or made the cycle complete.
No, if a body should ask you, you should tell him, I think, that the fall of a leaf, the pain of a bird, the hurt of a child, or a song, or a scowl, or a smile, or a word, make a difference.
That an ache in a lonely stranger's heart is an ache in a heart that is strange to him, that the joy that

the nuptial couple shares is the joy of lovers everywhere; that a sailor, dying alone at sea, is a song or a hope that is dying in me; that the drink to the thirsty, the hungry fed, the naked clothed, the weary to bed, that all we do, or leave undone, make a difference.

Ibid.

When you're lying awake with a dismal head-ache,
    and repose is taboo'd by anxiety,
I conceive you may use any language you choose
    to indulge in, without impropriety;
For your brain is on fire—the bedclothes conspire
    of usual slumber to plunder you:
First your counterpane goes, and uncovers your toes,
    and your sheet slips demurely from under you;
Then the blanketing tickles—you feel like mixed pickles—
    so terribly sharp is the pricking.
And you're hot, and you're cross, and you tumble and toss
    till there's nothing 'twixt you and the ticking.
Then the bedclothes all creep to the ground in a heap,
    and you pick 'em all up in a tangle;
Next your pillow resigns and politely declines
    to remain at its usual angle!
Well, you get some repose in the form of a doze,
    with hot eye-balls and head ever aching.
But your slumbering teems with such horrible dreams
    that you'd very much better be waking;
You're a regular wreck, with a crick in your neck,
    and no wonder you snore, for your head's on the floor,
    and you've needles and pins from your soles to your shins,

and your flesh is a-creep, for your left leg's asleep,
and you've cramp in your toes, and a fly on your nose,
and some fluff in your lung, and a feverish tongue,
and a thirst that's intense, and a general sense that you haven't been sleeping in clover;
But the darkness has passed, and it's daylight at last,
and the night has been long—ditto ditto my song—
and thank goodness they're both of them over!
Sir W. S. Gilbert, *Iolanthe*.

Long, too long America,
Traveling roads all even and peaceful
you learn'd from joys and prosperity only,
But now, ah now, to learn from crises of anguish,
advancing, grappling with direst fate and recoiling not,
And now to conceive and show to the world
what your children en-masse really are,
(For who except myself has yet conceiv'd what
your children en-masse really are?)
Walt Whitman, "Long, Too Long America"

Years of the modern! years of the unperform'd!
Your horizon rises, I see it parting away for more august dramas,
I see not America only, not only Liberty's nation but other nations preparing,

I see tremendous entrances and exits, new combinations, the solidarity of races,
I see that force advancing with irresistible power on the world's stage,
(Have the old forces, the old wars, played their parts? are the acts suitable to them closed?)
I see Freedom, completely arm'd and victorious and very haughty, with Law on one side and Peace on the other,
A stupendous trio all issuing forth against the idea of caste;
What historic denouements are these we so rapidly approach?
I see men marching and countermarching by swift millions,
I see the frontiers and boundaries of the old aristocracies broken,
I see the landmarks of European kings removed,
I see this day the People beginning their landmarks, (all others give way;)
Never were such sharp questions ask'd as this day,
Never was average man, his soul, more energetic, more like a God,
Lo, how he urges and urges, leaving the masses no rest!
His daring foot is on land and sea everywhere, he colonizes the Pacific, the archipelagoes,
With the steamship, the electric telegraph, the newspaper, the wholesale engines of war,
With these and the world-spreading factories he interlinks all geography, all lands;
What whispers are these O lands, running ahead of you, passing under the seas?
Are all nations communing? is there going to be but one heart to the globe?

Is humanity forming en-masse? for lo, tyrants tremble,
       crowns grow dim,
The earth, restive, confronts a new era, perhaps a general
       divine war,
No one knows what will happen next, such portents fill
       the days and nights;
Years prophetical! the space ahead as I walk, as I vainly
       try to pierce it, is full of phantoms,
Unborn deeds, things soon to be, project their shapes
       around me,
This incredible rush and heat, this strange ecstatic fever
       of dreams O years!
Your dreams O years, how they penetrate through me!
       (I know not whether I sleep or wake;)
The perform'd America and Europe grow dim, retiring
       in shadow behind me,
The unperform'd, more gigantic than ever, advance, advance upon me.
       Walt Whitman, "Years of the Modern"

LEADER OF CHORUS. Titititititi. What news do you bring?
EPOPS. Something that concerns our common safety, and is good news as well. Two men have come here to speak with me.
LEADER. Men? Here? Now? Do you know what you are saying?
EPOPS. Of course. I said, two old men have come from the realm of humans to suggest a great and wonderful plan to us.
LEADER. This is a horrible, unheard-of thing! What have you done to us?

EPOPS. I have welcomed two men, who wish to join us.
LEADER. You have dared to do such a thing!
EPOPS. Yes, and I am pleased at having done so.
LEADER. Are they already here?
EPOPS. They are.
CHORUS. Oh, woe, woe! We have been betrayed! Betrayed by one of us who picked up corn-kernels in the same fields as ourselves. He has broken our ancient laws; he has violated the oaths that bind all birds; he has given us over to the attacks of that wretched race which has always warred against us.
LEADER. These two old men shall be torn to pieces at once; the traitor among us shall be dealt with later.
PITHETAERUS. Did you hear that? We're finished!
EUELPIDES. And it's all your fault! Why did you bring me here?
PITHETAERUS. So I wouldn't be alone.
EUELPIDES. It's enough to make a man weep.
PITHETAERUS. Don't be ridiculous. How will you weep with your eyes pecked out?
CHORUS. Io! io! forward into battle, throw yourselves upon the enemy, spill his blood, take to your wings and surround them on all sides! Woe to them! Let us get to work with our beaks, let us consume them! Nothing can save them from our anger—not the mountains, the forests, the sky, nor the raging sea!

       Aristophanes, *The Birds*

CHORUS OF OLD MEN. Softly, softly! Our shoulders are sore from these miserable heavy olive stocks. But on we go, friends. What unexpected things do happen! Here we have the women daring to take over the Acropolis.

Let's hurry there; let's lay our fire-wood all about the citadel, and burn these wretched women, every one. Never, never will we let them laugh at us while we have life left in our bodies. These miserable women—can we not find some way to stop their incredible insolence? Let us press forward; we are almost there. Blow on the fire lest it go out just when we need it. Heavens, what a dreadful smoke! Ah, now it's burning brightly. If they still resist, we will set fire to the place and smoke them out. Help us, O gods; help us punish these audacious women who have taken our citadel.

CHORUS OF WOMEN. Ah! We see fire and smoke; what danger is this? To the water-pots! Good, we have them full now. Hurry, hurry! Take the water to our women comrades who are being threatened. A throng of ancient, doddering greybeards, issuing dreadful threats, are shrieking that they will cremate the women. Dear goddess Athene, we would see Athens and Greece cured of their warlike folly. Be of assistance, dear goddess, and help us to bring water to extinguish the fires of these old fools.

CHORUS OF MEN. What's this, what's this? A crowd of women outside to defend the gates! Come, men, let's knock out a few of their teeth and stop their braying.

CHORUS OF WOMEN. Come on! We're waiting for you. We dare you to touch us!

CHORUS OF MEN. And if we do, what will you do?

CHORUS OF WOMEN. We will tear you to bits with our teeth!

CHORUS OF MEN. Euripides was right when he said that woman is the most shameless of beasts!

CHORUS OF WOMEN. Now to our water jars.

CHORUS OF MEN. You stupid women, what do you expect to do here with your water?

CHORUS OF WOMEN. And you, old men, with your fire? Will you cremate yourselves?
CHORUS OF MEN. Build up the fire, men, we'll roast the old hags!
CHORUS OF WOMEN. To our pots, women, to our pots! Let's do our duty. We're watering you, old men, to bring back your youthful bloom!
CHORUS OF MEN. We're all wet! What insolence! What insolence!

Aristophanes, Lysistrata

CHORUS. Of the wonders of the world, none is more wonderful than man; he has the power to cross the white-capped sea, to stand against the storm-filled south wind, and to plough from year to year the brown soil of Earth.
ONE VOICE. Excelling in cunning, he entraps the birds of the forest.
ONE VOICE. With his nets he catches the quick and shining fishes from the sea.
ONE VOICE. Because of man's patience, the wild bull and the horse become his servants.
ONE VOICE. The beasts, roaming in the woods, are subject to his traps.
ONE VOICE. Man taught himself speech, and the processes of thought.
ONE VOICE. Protection from the icy rain and from the blazing, merciless sun man has secured for himself.
CHORUS. Death alone he cannot master. Nor always the consequence of his thoughts. Only from thoughts that are honourable and just will come honour and justice to his city.

Sophocles, Antigone

PROMETHEUS. You see me as I am
A god condemned by God,
Condemned to suffer pain
Ten thousand years in chains.
Yet all that you behold
I have beheld before,
Knowing this time would come,
This time of punishment.
I gave to mortal man
The right of men to think.
I brought to man the light
The light of heavenly fire.
This is my awesome crime,
The great Promethean sin.
Thus, for my gift to earth,
I am earthbound and yoked.
Excessive in my love,
My love for mortal man,
I reap the wrath of God.
CHORUS. What god among the gods
Finds joy in your torment?
Who on Olympian heights
Finds pleasure in your pain?
PROMETHEUS. Fearless I speak his name
and cry defiantly,
Defiant of his will,
The will of Zeus himself.
CHORUS. The will of Zeus? Beware.
PROMETHEUS. Yet there shall come a time
When he shall need my mind,
And there will come a day
When he will need my love.
Yet, hear what I proclaim:
When that day comes, I swear

I'll not be coaxed or cowed
To tell him what I know,
Or give him love for wrath
Until he sets me free.
CHORUS. Beware, Prometheus,
Beware of what you say.
The curse of Zeus is just.
How can you question that?
PROMETHEUS. I question everything,
Because I gave to man
The right of questioning.
I gave to man the right
To hope and to believe.
I brought enlightenment
To all the darkened earth,
And taught mankind to sing
A song transcending doom.
CHORUS. What you have done seems good,
Good in the sight of man;
But in the sight of God—
PROMETHEUS. What, in the sight of God?
What in God's sight is wrong?
CHORUS. Only the gods know that
And you, a god, should know.
PROMETHEUS. Blind, blind . . . still woefully blind . . .
Still in the dark you dwell.
When will men claim the right
To reason in the light?
CHORUS. When will you face your fault,
And when repent your sin?
PROMETHEUS. You ask me to repent?
You, standing there secure,
Free and secure from pain.

Easy enough to say
Repent . . . easy enough
When you are not in chains.
But I, whose only sin
Was helping man, am bound.
CHORUS. We grieve for you. We weap,
But mighty Zeus must rule,
So you are thus enslaved.
PROMETHEUS. I tell you God himself
Will fail, if he will not
Learn that rule and slavery
Are not one and the same.
CHORUS. You wish the death of God?
PROMETHEUS. I wish for life for man,
And wish for light and love,
And for a god of love.
CHORUS. You are the enemy
The enemy of Zeus.
PROMETHEUS. I am the enemy
Of all that hinders man.
CHORUS. Your words proclaim you mad.
PROMETHEUS. Yes, if it is madness
To seek to light the world.
To bring that light, I live.
I suffer and I live.
The thundering storm descends,
The lightning strikes and burns.
I suffer through for man,
I Prometheus,
I suffer through for man.

> Aeschylus, *Prometheus Bound,*
> free translation by Albert
> Johnson

ELECTRA. Ah, pure sunlight, and clear air, earth's canopy, how often have you heard my sad lament. I beg the gods to listen to my weeping, and help me to avenge the murder of my dear father. My strength is waning fast, and my grief is more than I can bear.

CHORUS OF WOMEN. Electra, pitiful daughter of a pitiless mother, do not spend your young days in grieving for one who has gone. True it is that your brave and honourable father was murdered by your faithless mother's mate Aegisthus, but your weeping will not bring Agamemnon back to life.

ELECTRA. Dear friends, to soothe and comfort me you have come. I welcome you. The love you bring to me I give to you. But entreat me not to cease my weeping. My sorrow is too deep.

CHORUS OF WOMEN. We know how deep is your sorrow, and would that we might ease it. But Agamemnon, that fine and just man, your father, cannot return from the land of the dead.

ELECTRA. Only a heart of stone would not grieve. Only an unfeeling mind could forget. No. My heart will turn to the nightingale, sad bird of grief; and I will pray to Niobe, Queen of Sorrow.

CHORUS OF WOMEN. You were not alone, dear Electra, with this burden of grief. Your sisters who live within, and your brother, Orestes, though exiled—they too mourned for your father. And do not fear, my child, that Orestes will not return. He will come, with the help of Zeus, and find welcome and honour in this, his land.

ELECTRA. That too is part of my sorrow. I have grown weary with waiting. Days and years have gone by. I have waited, unwedded and childless, waited for Orestes, but he does not come. He knows of this, he knows of my sorrow, but he does not come. He sends messages, but he does not come.

CHORUS OF WOMEN. Take courage, my child, take courage. Great Zeus is still king in the heavens. He sees and rules all. Leave to him this bitter quarrel, and temper the hatred that is in your heart. Time has the power to heal your wound. And you must believe that Orestes will come. He will not forget his father.

ELECTRA. So much of my life has been lived in despair. My weariness overcomes me as I stand here alone, with none to share the burden—no husband or children to comfort me. And like a slave, despised by all, I must serve in the house of my father!

CHORUS OF WOMEN. Child, child, turn this bitterness from your soul. Such brooding will destroy you.

ELECTRA. I know this, as I know my own passion. But while I live, I will not change. Did you truly think you could comfort me? Do not try further, my friends. I can never know a respite from my sorrows, or a limit to my grief.

CHORUS OF WOMEN. It is with love, Electra, that we beg you not to add woe to woe.

ELECTRA. How can it be right to neglect the dead? If the killer pay not with blood for blood, then all regard for man, all fear of heaven, will vanish from the earth.

Sophocles, *Electra*

Tiger, Tiger

Tiger, tiger, burning bright
In the forests of the night,
What immortal hand or eye
Could frame thy fearful symmetry?

In what distant deeps or skies
Burnt the fire of thine eyes?
On what wings dare he aspire?
What the hand dare seize the fire?

And what shoulder and what art
Could twist the sinews of thy heart?
And, when thy heart began to beat,
What dread hand and what dread feet?

What the hammer? What the chain?
In what furnace was thy brain?
What the anvil? What dread grasp
Dare its deadly terrors clasp?

When the stars threw down their spears,
And water'd heaven with their tears,
Did He smile His work to see?
Did He who made the lamb make thee?

Tiger, tiger, burning bright
In the forests of the night,
What immortal hand or eye
Dare frame thy fearful symmetry?
                              William Blake

Last Lines

No coward soul is mine,
No trembler in the world's storm-troubled sphere:
I see Heaven's glories shine,
And faith shines equal, arming me from fear.

O God within my breast,
Almighty, ever-present Deity!
Life—that in me has rest,
As I—undying Life—have power in Thee!

Vain are the thousand creeds
That move men's hearts: unutterably vain;
Worthless as wither'd weeds,
Or idlest froth amid the boundless main,

To waken doubt in one
Holding so fast by Thine Infinity;
So surely anchor'd on
The steadfast rock of immortality.

With wide-embracing love
Thy Spirit animates eternal years,
Pervades and broods above,
Changes, sustains, dissolves, creates, and rears.

Though earth and man were gone,
And suns and universes ceased to be,
And Thou were left alone,
Every existence would exist in Thee.

There is not room for Death,
Nor atom that his might could render void:
Thou—Thou art Being and Breath,
And what Thou art may never be destroyed.
                              Emily Brontë

Uphill

Does the road wind uphill all the way?
Yes, to the very end.
Will the day's journey take the whole long day?
From morn to night, my friend.

But is there for the night a resting-place?
A roof for when the slow, dark hours begin.
May not the darkness hide it from my face?
You cannot miss that inn.

Shall I meet other wayfarers at night?
Those who have gone before.
Then must I knock, or call when just in sight?
They will not keep you waiting at that door.

Shall I find comfort, travel-sore and weak?
Of labour you shall find the sum.
Will there be beds for me and all who seek?
Yea, beds for all who come.
      Christina Georgina Rossetti

The Night Has a Thousand Eyes

The night has a thousand eyes,
And the day but one;
Yet the light of the bright world dies
With the dying sun.

The mind has a thousand eyes,
And the heart but one;
Yet the light of a whole life dies
When love is done.
     Francis William Bourdillon

Chill of the Eve

A long green swell
Slopes soft to the sea;
And a far-off bell
Swings sweet to me;
As the grey
Chill day
Slips away
From the lea.

Spread cold and far,
Without one glow
From a mild pale star,
Is the sky's steel bow;
And the grey
Chill day
Slips away
Below.

Yon green tree grieves
To the air around;
And the whispering leaves
Have a lonely sound;
As the grey
Chill day
Slips away
From the ground.

And dark, more dark,
The shades settle down;
Far off is a spark
From the lamp-lit town;
And the grey
Chill day
Slips away
With a frown.
                    James Stephens

A Word

A word is dead
When it is said,
Some say.
I say it just
Begins to live
That day.
            Emily Dickinson

Jabberwocky

'Twas brillig, and the slithy toves
Did gyre and gimble in the wabe:
All mimsy were the borogoves,
And the mome raths outgrabe.

"Beware the Jabberwock, my son!
The jaws that bite, the claws that catch!
Beware the Jubjub bird, and shun
The frumious Bandersnatch!"

He took his vorpal sword in hand;
Long time the manxome foe he sought—
So rested he by the Tumtum tree,
And stood awhile in thought.

And, as in uffish thought he stood,
The Jabberwock, with eyes of flame,
Came whiffling through the tulgey wood,
And burbled as it came!

One, two! One, two! And through and through
The vorpal blade went snicker-snack!
He left it dead, and with its head
He went galumphing back.

"And hast thou slain the Jabberwock?
Come to my arms, my beamish boy!
O frabjous day! Callooh, Callay!"
He chortled in his joy.

'Twas brillig, and the slithy toves
Did gyre and gimble in the wabe:
All mimsy were the borogoves,
And the mome raths outgrabe.

                                        Lewis Carroll

From The Pied Piper of Hamelin

And out of the houses the rats came tumbling,
Great rats, small rats, lean rats, brawny rats,
Brown rats, black rats, gray rats, tawny rats,
Grave old plodders, gay young friskers,
Fathers, mothers, uncles, cousins,
Cocking tails and pricking whiskers,
Families by tens and dozens,
Brothers, sisters, husbands, wives—
Followed the Piper for their lives.

                          Robert Browning

Dover Beach

The sea is calm tonight.
The tide is full, the moon lies fair
Upon the straits;—on the French coast the light
Gleams and is gone; the cliffs of England stand
Glimmering and vast, out in the tranquil bay.
Come to the window, sweet is the night-air!
Only, from the long line of spray
Where the sea meets the moon-blanched land,
Listen! you hear the grating roar
Of pebbles which the waves draw back, and fling,
At their return, up the high strand,
Begin, and cease, and then again begin,
With tremulous cadence slow, and bring
The eternal note of sadness in.

Sophocles long ago
Heard it on the Aegean, and it brought
Into his mind the turbid ebb and flow
Of human misery; we
Find also in the sound a thought,
Hearing it by this distant northern sea.

The Sea of Faith
Was once, too, at the full, and round earth's shore
Lay like the folds of a bright girdle furled.
But now I only hear
Its melancholy, long, withdrawing roar,
Retreating, to the breath
Of the night-wind, down the vast edges drear
And naked shingles of the world.

Ah, love, let us be true
To one another! for the world, which seems
To lie before us like a land of dreams,
So various, so beautiful, so new,
Hath really neither joy, nor love, nor light,
Nor certitude, nor peace, nor help for pain;
And we are here as on a darkling plain
Swept with confused alarms of struggle and flight,
Where ignorant armies clash by night.
                                        Matthew Arnold

Before the Beginning of Years

Before the beginning of years
There came to the making of man
Time, with a gift of tears;
Grief, with a glass that ran;

Pleasure, with pain for leaven;
Summer, with flowers that fell;
Remembrance fallen from heaven,
And madness risen from hell;

Strength without hands to smite;
Love that endures for a breath;
Night, the shadow of light,
And life, the shadow of death.

And the high gods took in hand
Fire, and the falling of tears,
And a measure of sliding sand
From under the feet of the years;

And froth and drift of the sea;
And dust of the labouring earth;
And bodies of things to be
In the houses of death and of birth;

And wrought with weeping and laughter,
And fashion'd with loathing and love,
With life before and after
And death beneath and above,

For a day and a night and a morrow,
That his strength might endure for a span
With travail and heavy sorrow,
The holy spirit of man

From the winds of the north and the south
They gather'd as unto strife;
They breathed upon his mouth,
They filled his body with life;

Eyesight and speech they wrought
For the veils of the soul therein,
A time for labour and thought,
A time to serve and to sin;

They gave him light in his ways,
And love, and a space for delight,
And beauty and length of days,
And night, and sleep in the night.

His speech is a burning fire;
With his lips he travaileth;
In his heart is a blind desire,
In his eyes foreknowledge of death;

He weaves, and is clothed with derision;
Sows, and he shall not reap;
His life is a watch or a vision
Between a sleep and a sleep.

     Algernon Charles Swinburne

Regarding readers' theatre, we should first regard its vague and ramified definition. Just what do people mean when they talk about readers theatre? The truth is, they mean so many different things that our best approach might be to clarify some of the different meanings. It seems that readers theatre can be anything from an ad hoc group spontaneously assembled to read a play either for an audience or for their own amusement to a company of well-trained, well-rehearsed actors presenting a reading performance in which they walk through the stage blocking and execute the stage business with some detail, yet give the appearance of reading from the script which they carry in hand. A readers' theatre may consist of a few people who get together casually to read a play for their own pleasure without benefit of an audience, or of an organized group which meets regularly to perform for an audience. It may also consist of various people called together from time to time who sit around a table and read a play for a few of their friends. It may be a group that gets together spontaneously without a director, or it may be several different groups working with several different directors, or it may be a project that is close to a finished public production. Whatever it is, it is definitely a part of corporate reading, and were there no other reason, it deserves our attention for that alone. However, there are other reasons that arrest our attention. Some of those reasons were indicated in the early paragraphs of this chapter. Other reasons may be even more significant.

Though some may be reluctant to admit it, most people love to act. Virtually every human being is born with some degree of acting instinct. Much of acting is imitating, and every normal baby is born with an ability to imitate. If this were not so he would never learn. He learns to smile, to walk, to talk, by imitating. When he grows to childhood he enters that world of make-believe. A little girl pretends she is mommy, a nurse, a fairy godmother. A little boy pretends he is a cowboy, an Indian, an astronaut, or the funny man on television. Somewhere along the way we become self-conscious and thwart our inclinations to pretend, but the old endemic desire to act is usually lurking somewhere in the subconscious. It is good to act. It is a great way to work off inhibitions, hostilities, and frustrations. It is a marvelous medium for self-expression, self-renewal, and self-revelation. It is a medium in which we get to know ourselves and others to an extent we cannot realize in any other way. Acting is good, and everyone who can should do it.

Readers' theatre provides an opportunity for all those people who cannot or will not give the time which regular theatre demands. It is a godsend to all frustrated hams. Who in his histrionic heart is not a ham? So for such as these, readers theatre as defined above is a playhouse.

However, readers' theatre serves another purpose. In fact, it serves at least two other purposes. It is a laboratory for young actors and directors as well as playwrights, and it affords a novel entertainment for theatre buffs.

Whether the readers' theatre is an auxiliary to or substitution for the full-scale theatre program, it is a great boon to young actors always eager for all the acting experience they can get. In cases where the readers' theatre is open to a cross-section of the community's citizenry, young actors are often given a chance to perform with people who are more mature and may have had more experience. The plays that are chosen for a readers' theatre can usually be selected from a much wider spectrum than is the case when budgets, set construction, and box office revenue are a consideration. This flexibility means that new scripts and experimental plays can be included in the schedule.

Young directors who are not yet quite ready to try their wings on a full-scale production can serve their apprenticeships in readers' theatre. Likewise, those students whose primary interests in drama is the oral interpretation of the text find an ideal medium in readers' theatre. Furthermore, works of unusual literary merit that might prove too esoteric for the regular theatre patrons can be brought to life in the readers theatre. Many great plays which are considered museum pieces might remain buried in the archives indefinitely were it not for readers' theatre. Similarly, directors can have a fling at vanguard forms that might be considered too far out for the general public.

To the student interested in playwriting, the readers' theatre is a veritable workshop. Since this book deals with the creative as well as the interpretive aspects of oral communication, this is a feature not to be overlooked. Since most people subscribe to the theory that a play is not a play until it has been performed, the readers' theatre fills a vital need for those creative minds who want to have a fling at playwriting. Once a new script has had a try-out in readers' theatre, the author is in a position to make revisions based on empirical knowledge.

Readers' theatre often appeals to a particular breed of playgoer, including people who are not habitual playgoers at all. The regular theatre patrons who are curious about rare plays or who like to keep abreast of the "In" thing, or who are interested in anything and everything theatrical, will likely be among those who attend the readers' theatre. However, readers' theatre has a special appeal all its own, and it is almost certain to attract students, faculty members, and townspeople who like the idea of hearing a play read and enjoy being in on an event which to them seems quite novel. The fact that a readers' theatre can be held almost anywhere at almost any time means that the theatre can be taken to the audience rather than the other way around. The student lounge, a classroom, a dormitory living room, a shady spot on the campus, or even a designated area in the downtown mall can be a suitable place for a readers' theatre performance.

There are a few specific techniques that are applicable to readers' theatre. Let us conclude this chapter on corporate reading with a brief discussion of those techniques. We should begin by recognizing that one of the major elements in drama is usually missing in readers theatre. That element is spectacle. It is missing because the emphasis is usually on the oral and literary elements rather than the visual aspects.

This being true, the techniques that are called for are suggested in the following guidelines:

1. The reader must know the play, not merely his own role. He must understand thoroughly his relation to all the other characters and what his role contributes to the total play. He should know the premise, the argument, the crisis, and the climax.

2. Since he has no visual aid to assist him other than his face, it is incumbent on the reader to project the play by voice alone. This involves projection, articulation, and an intelligent use of all the elements of interpretation. He must never forget that he, as actor, is helping to tell the story of the play to the audience.

3. A reading performance, like any other performance, calls for complete concentration. This means the reader must always remain in character when he is on stage. He should read in character, listen in character, and react in

character. Any wandering of attention or breaking up over a laugh line is, it should go without saying, strictly taboo.

4. The performance will be greatly enhanced if the reader can lift his eyes from the script frequently and focus his eyes on the person to whom he is talking or to whom he is listening. Readers who are script-bound or who keep their faces down are usually deadly dull. The idea is to make the play a living experience with voice, face, and mind.

5. Such things as posture, stance, emotional integrity, and mood are matters that must be kept in mind. One actor forgetting these basics momentarily can mar and even wreck the performance. A reader performing in a readers' theatre, irrespective of the size of his role, should perform as though the performance depended on him and him alone. In a vital sense it does.

In conclusion, let us say that corporate reading in any and all of its various forms is basically a group experience. In terms of art it is a group expression. The group becomes a performing unit, an organism with virtually a life of its own. It is the impact of the group that counts. That impact will be as significant as the group is capable of making it. However, the group, let us never forget, is made up of individuals. It is the loyalty, dedication, concentration, unselfishness, trust, and love of the individual that determine the character, the power, and the artistry of the group.

7

Creative Thinking: The Primal Impetus

If we appear to be limiting the creative aspect of oral communication to this single final chapter, let us think back through the preceding pages. It should be discovered that much of what we have covered belongs as much or more in the creative column as on the interpretive side of the page. Some consideration of the creative approach is implicit in each chapter. Indeed, interpretation itself involves the creative process quite as much as technical know-how. Why, then, this chapter?

The why is in the term *creative thinking*. There is a new and urgent need for creative thinking. The need has always existed, but in this time of multiple explosions, when everyone is having to learn so much so fast, the need becomes an ultimatum. Either we learn to think creatively or knowledge will avail us nothing but oblivion. The ghettos will get us, the cost of law and order will bankrupt us, starvation will strangle us, polution will dispossess us, or the computers will take command, and there is still and seemingly forever the Bomb. Can we who hold this good, green earth, keep it fit for life, and fill it with the life it challenges?

Is the answer to these questions in creative thinking? It may be, if that word *creative* is constructively conceived. It is true that men may create evil things, but, before we bog down in semantics, let us explain that we think of creativity in contrast to its antonyms, destruction and annihilation. We use the word *creativity* as expressed in the Webster's Dictionary phrase, *an act of grace*. We mean it as an act of goodness as in the Genesis sense, *God created*.

So, then, to think creatively means to come up with new ideas that, in our best judgment, will make things better for all breathing life. Man's judgment is not infallible, to be sure, but if with all our hearts we search for truth, and fresh, original ways of expressing truth, we will at least be doing what we can do, and as Anouilh says in his play *Antigone,* "What a person can do, a person ought to do."

Fresh ways to penetrate the past and probe the future, to correlate new knowledge relating it to life, fresh ways of fostering reconciliation of men with men and man with nature, and fresh, new, exciting ways of finding new depths of meaning in the treasure of our heritage and great revelation in words waiting to be written and proclaimed, these are the ends for which creative thinking is a means. The means are in us, with us, all about us. The means are deep in nearly every mind, but every mind, alas, cannot unlock the treasure chest of marvels deeply immersed in the strata of the subconscious. Yet everyone can do more than he probably thinks he can. There are techniques for reaching the unremembered wisdom of our minds. There are techniques for capturing those ideas which Thomas Edison insisted filled the air. Let us examine those techniques and then go on to tell of a few creative projects we have had the good fortune to observe.

Here follow some tried and proven exercises designed to contribute toward creative thinking.

1. Wait. Sit still and wait. Waiting is not easy. Sitting still is not easy. The moment you sit down to wait you'll think of a hundred things you ought to be doing. Put them out of your mind. That may be difficult, but try. Keep trying, and don't fidget as you try. Discipline yourself to sit still and wait. Mental discipline is a first step to creativity.

2. Stop thinking. This will be even harder than sitting still. Just try thinking of nothing and see how impossible it is. Is it really impossible? No, but you will probably swear it is the first few times you try. Practice making your mind a perfect blank. Hindus do it. Why shouldn't you? You should. It is part of the discipline. Practice your concentration on nothingness until you can extend the interval to several seconds.

3. Day dream. We don't mean the kind of day dreaming one does in anticipation of a party, a game, a dance, or some special event. Simply relax and let ideas flow through your mind at random. Exercise your mind in free association. Caution! Negative thoughts are out of bounds. Reject resentment, fear, animosity, hostility, anxiety. Let only good, strong, positive thoughts flood through your mind, and, as they do this, enjoy them. Joy is the bride of creativity.

4. Study an object. Select a pencil, a button, a medallion, a flower, a leaf, or any single item and sit regarding it. Focus your mind completely on the object, directing your thoughts only to the object. Study its form, its size, its color. See how many things you can see in it that you have never seen before. Relate the object to yourself, your needs, your use of it, your feeling toward it,

5. Read and reflect. Find a poem, philosophical statement, some verses of scripture, or a choice piece of literature and read with many stops. Stop after every thought that is expressed and reflect on what it says. Do not read critically. This is not a study in criticism. Instead, read with appreciation. Read for the purpose of stimulating your own thinking. Read for enjoyment. Reflect with rejoicing.

Mastery of the above exercises, ideal as it would be, will not come all at once. They should be taken one at a time, with several days to each. A short time each day should be devoted to this venture, but one should be consistent in the daily drill. After several days, when the exercise is well under control, two or more may be combined until all five are practiced at a single sitting. All of this is merely by way of disciplining the mind for creative thinking.

The object of creative thinking is to create something. At least that is one of the objects. There is another of equal importance which we will discuss later. The next step is to concentrate on the thing to be created.

First there is the problem of deciding on just what it is that is to be created. Is it a poem, a play, a short story, a novel, a scenario, a T.V. script, some audio-visual project, or an invention of some sort? Or is it an original class project, a fresh approach to a reading or a role? Or perhaps it is a song, a painting, a piece of sculpture, a free-form ceramic, or a mobile. Whatever it is, it is selected, eventually, out of several possibilities. The period of selection may go on for days or weeks or even months. Creative matters cannot be forced with too much pressure. However, there comes at last that moment of decision.

Once the decision is made there should be no deviation, no shilly-shallying, no wondering if some other choice might have been better. This does not mean that an idea might not be abandoned in favor of something else eventually, but such a change in objective should be indulged only after a serious investment of time has been directed toward the first choice. One should abandon a creative project only when he is convinced that he has a better idea.

Once the creative idea is definitely chosen, it should become something of an *idée fixe*. It should possess the creator and he should happily let it possess him. The idea will haunt him day and night, and each time he finds it entering his conscious mind, even when he is busy with other things, he should let it come with no resentment. A creative idea must be treated as a very dear friend, or even a lover. One must learn to say to the idea something like "Good. Welcome. Don't leave me, ever. I don't have time to give you my full attention just now, but we'll get together soon." Ideas, like children, have to be wanted. Otherwise they become alienated and difficult to manage.

There may be some question about this matter of management. Does the person with the creative idea do the managing, or is he actually managed by the creative idea? Sometimes an idea is so powerful that it seems to burst full blown into a creation with little assistance and not so much as a labor pain. Still, short or long, there has to be a period of maturation.

It is during the maturation that nourishment must be given to the idea. This may consist of reading for background, listening to music, researching definite related matters, or talking the idea over with friends.

However, talking about the idea is dangerous. Many writers, for instance, never talk about their current project. It is so easy to talk the idea out, thus denying it a proper birth. It is easier for most people to talk than to write, and always easier to talk big about what one plans to do than to get down to business and do it. So, while the creative idea is in incubation it is best to talk about other things and keep the idea itself a deep, dark, devastating secret.

Comes the day when the secret is out and the idea is happily born. Bells can ring and the announcement can be widely proclaimed. Rarely, however, is a creative idea born with full maturity. It comes in the nature of a first, rough draft, or a kind of trial run. Revisions are as inevitable as they are desirable, and a certain amount of honing, shaping, and polishing is always necessary, often for weeks or months. It is simply part of the creative business.

It has been observed time and again that creative people are dynamic, receptive, and youthful. Some of our most prolific artists have enjoyed longevity, but when they have continued to be productive they have retained their youthful quality. This is evidenced in the creativity of such people as Arturo Toscanini, Johann Bach, Leopold Stokowski, Robert Frost, Thomas Edison, and the venerable George Bernard Shaw. The creative act seems to keep people vibrant and active. Perhaps it is the creative point of view that does it. In any event it is that creative point of view which we want to discuss next.

Problems are for solving. People with a creative viewpoint believe that. Such persons tackle a problem head on. They are not beaten before they start. Every problem, great or small, is accepted as a challenge. To them problem-solving is a kind of game.

Thus we see that creative thinking is not an esoteric activity for which the artists hold a monopoly. Quite the contrary is true. Executives, administrators, legislators, and people in all the professions may be and should be creative, in spite of the fact that many of them, sadly enough, often are not. Clearly, the creative attitude is for all who will train themselves to acquire it. It is not for the fainthearted, the quitters, the defeatists, and the pessimists. It is not for them, but it is a means by which they may experience a metamorphosis.

The very fact that a creative attitude can change people is one more argument for stressing the importance of creative thinking in this treatise on oral communication. Students are in the process of change. Change is their business. If they weren't interested in change, they wouldn't be students. They would be dropouts, casualties who gave up on themselves and society, disillusioned and convinced that things will never get any better.

Students know that the one unchanging certainty is change itself. Change is inevitable. The question is not whether or not there will be changes, but what kind of changes do we anticipate? Will they be changes for good, or for ill, for better, or for worse? The inescapable answer is, "both."

Next question—what kind of changes do we want? Do we want change merely for the sake of change? Do we want the new just because it is new? Is the newest always synonymous with the best? Is the "In" thing necessarily our thing?

What kind of changes do we want in society and in ourselves? The nihilists protest that the Establishment must go. Go where? Go when? How go? Should the Establishment go, or should we try to make it a going concern? If it must go, then go for what? What takes its place?

Anarchists don't care. Down with everything, they cry. Thinking students do care. Thinking students care about themselves and about the civilization which they are fashioning. They care about change and ask, in fact demand, to know what changes they can effect and how they themselves can change to keep apace with change.

The questions and the quest go on, and on we go to try to keep abreast. At such a pace in such a race we need creative thinking. We need the drive of disciplined creative thought, need it at all levels, need it in solving problems space-size and personal. Seismic, titanic tasks lie just ahead. Meanwhile we train creatively to face them. As Hamlet says, "The readiness is all." The few creative projects we offer now are meant to be suggestion stimuli. None are earthshaking, none tremendous. They are but stepping-stones toward giant strides, those strides that may be taken if preparation is complete.

The creative projects briefly described below are taken from many classroom assignments in current courses.

1. *Myself in Verse.* Susan was in search of her identity, a search quite common among freshmen, and found she could let go in poetry reading. Then, while searching for a creative idea, she tried her hand at writing verse of her own. Her poems were intimate, personal, arresting. She arranged them in a program that was meant to illustrate her growth as a personality. It was not great verse but it did great things for Susan.

2. Charles, an interesting young renegade, found he could identify with the poetry of Dylan Thomas, so did a one-man show of *Under Milk Wood,* acting all the roles and handling the narration himself.

3. Inspired, no doubt, by Hal Holbrook's *Mark Twain Tonight,* Mike put together selections from *Huckleberry Finn* and *Tom Sawyer* and discovered an acting talent he didn't know he had. Subsequently he did a lot of acting.

4. Paula was a camera buff and Pete was good with a tape recorder. They worked together on a film strip of seascapes photographed along the California coast, showing the many moods of the Pacific, to which, by tape, Pete added tell-tale sound of surf, sea gulls, and fragments of appropriate verse.

5. Carl, also handy with the tape recorder, recorded a series of spooky, Hitchcockian sounds: wind wails, creaky doors, a screech owl; and did a rendition of cuttings from Poe's *House of Usher*. He had edited the tape so that the sounds come in precisely on cue.

6. Cindy, a Japanese girl from Hawaii, presented an ancient Japanese legend in which she spoke, sang, and danced. It was a little like a solo rendition of a Nōh play.

7. Debbie, preparing to teach first grade, presented three children's stories of her own creation. To give the presentation an original touch, she talked not to the class but to a doll, a panda, and a stuffed white rat fittingly arranged on stage.

8. Merle made a short, spectacular skiing film which he narrated in verse of his own creation. Both film and verse were spiced with humor.

We have cited only those creative projects that were suitable for a class in oral interpretation. Other creative projects include the writing of plays, short and full length, film scenarios, T.V. scripts, experiments in cinematography, the editing of sound tracks, film strips, and various other ventures. There is virtually no limit to the creative projects that can be conceived. The important thing is that each project have a point, a definite reason for being, and honest self-expression and a challenge to the creative imagination.

It is significant that the major foundations such as Ford and Rockefeller, as well as others, are giving priority to institutions and projects that are taking a bold, creative approach to education. It is significant, too, that no nation in history or the world has invested so heavily as the United States in the gamble on human intelligence. In this country we pour hundreds of billions of dollars into people, recognizing them to be our main resource. The investment is in the training of minds, the development of imagination and creativity, and the improvement of health. This investment is based on the premise that with such an investment in people, rather than in machinery and technology, the citizens will receive a much higher rate of interest on their dollar outlay. Thus far, though the venture is young, the prospect is promising.

Nearly two hundred years ago the Scottish political economist Adam Smith advanced the idea that a nation should take steps to see to it that its people are ingenious, sharp, and physically energetic. Investment in goods, material things, new industry, and real estate is all well and good, but secondary to the investment in the minds of the citizens. This contention is supported by such authorities as the nineteenth-century economist Alfred Marshall, who maintained that the most valuable of all capital is that which is invested in human beings.

That such philosophy is pragmatically sound is evidenced by the fact that during the past twenty years the United States has more than doubled its output of goods from three hundred billion to six hundred and fifty billion dollars. It is estimated by the joint economic committee of the United States Congress that by 1972 our national output will reach one trillion dollars. Such are the material rewards of dollar investment in the creative potentials of a nation's people. With only six percent of the world's population, the United States produces over thirty percent of the world's produce. Furthermore, in spite of our disgraceful pockets of poverty, it is estimated that at least one fourth of American families now realize an income of ten thousand dollars annually.

It should be inspiring to the creative mind to realize that thirty percent of our national physical capital is committed to education. It would be more inspiring if we could be assured of marked decrease in expenditures on defense, but nevertheless we have increased our annual investment in education from three billion to fifty-two billion dollars in the past thirty years. That figure refers only to chartered institutions. The amount invested annually is much, much more when private schools, on-the-job training, and educational television are included. The figure then is estimated at two hundred billion dollars.

Behind this vast empire of knowledge is creative thinking which cannot be evaluated in terms of monetary standards. Pertinent to the real evaluation is the fact that a quarter of our current population is now engaged in full-time education. That percentage, along with our investment in education, far exceeds all other nations in the world, though Japan and Soviet Russia are not too far behind. In our country, seventy-two percent of all our young people graduate from high school and approximately half of those go on to college.

The creative energy back of our knowledge explosion is evidenced in another spectacular way. In the past ten years alone our country has created again as much college and university capacity as has existed during the past three hundred years. During the same period attendance in institutions of higher learning has jetted from three million to seven million. With a thrust like this, creative imagination can well work around the clock.

Clearly the wealth of a nation must be measured in brain power quite as much as material power. Indeed it is that brain power that will make the difference between capitulation to disaster and possible annihilation and the great leap forward. Basic to this possible great leap forward is the interesting fact that all this recent advancement in knowledge has come about simply because parents have wanted a better deal for their children. The hope for the leap, then, lies in the children and in their matching desire to procure a better deal for their children. Will that happen? Most of the two million six hundred thousand members of the teaching profession are betting their careers that it will. Most of some seven million students are betting that way too. The bet is more than a gamble. It is a faith. It is a faith in human potentials. It is a faith based on the revelation of human excellence. Talent, intelligence, creativity, and the desire to excel are the potent elements in the new capital, the new wealth of the nation.

It may be that the advancement of the human race lies not in technological achievement and material wealth but in the creative mind of man himself.

The world has raced forward rapidly since the days of Karl Marx who, a hundred years ago, conceived of capital as the ownership of the means of production, namely, the raw materials, tools, land, and so on, from which wealth was created. Were Marx alive today he might be the first to see that capital is also the initiative, industry, character, and creative power of man himself, and that the new capital is something more intangible than materials. He might see what wise men of the century are seeing—that the new capital is really the power of men to think creatively.

Appendix

Selections for Creative and Interpretive Reading

Narrative Poetry

Samuel Taylor Coleridge, "The Rime of the Ancient Mariner"
Anonymous, "Bonny Barbara Allan"
Anonymous, "Barbara Allen's Cruelty"
Anonymous, "Lord Randal"
Anonymous, "The Unquiet Grave"
Anonymous, "The Falcon"
Anonymous, "The Three Ravens"
Tristram Coffin, "The Race"
Robert Frost, "The Death of the Hired Man"
Stephen Vincent Benet, "John Brown's Body"
Edna St. Vincent Millay, "The Ballad of the Harp Weaver"
E. A. Robinson, "Richard Cory"
A. E. Housman, "The True Lover"
Geoffrey Chaucer, "The Pardoner's Tale"
Robert Frost, "The Impulse"

Dramatic Poetry

Thomas Hardy, "New Year's Eve"
John Donne, "The Funeral"
Alfred, Lord Tennyson, "Ulysses"
Robert Browning, "My Last Duchess"
Amy Lowell, "Patterns"
e. e. cummings, "sweet let me go"
James Weldon Johnson, "The Creation"
Edgar Lee Masters, selections from *Spoon River Anthology*
Andrew Marvell, "To His Coy Mistress"
A. E. Housman, "Is My Team Ploughing"
A. E. Housman, "To an Athlete Dying Young"
Emily Dickinson, "I Died for Beauty"
Walter de la Mare, "The Listeners"
D. H. Lawrence, "Love on the Farm"
George Gordon, Lord Byron, "The Prisoner of Chillon"
T. S. Eliot, "Portrait of a Lady"
Robert Browning, "Soliloquy of the Spanish Cloister"
John Keats, "The Eve of St. Agnes"
Robert Bridges, "I Will Not Let Thee Go"
John Donne, "The Good-Morrow"
John Crowe Ransom, "Piazza Piece"
Michael Drayton, "Since There's No Help . . ."

Lyric Poetry

T. S. Eliot, "The Love Song of J. Alfred Prufrock"
Robert Frost, "The Impulse"
John Donne, "The Legacy"
Elizabeth Barrett Browning, "How Do I Love Thee . . ."
Percy Bysshe Shelley, "Ode to the West Wind"
John Keats, "Ode to a Nightingale"
Dante Gabriel Rossetti, "The Blessed Damozel"

John Masefield, "Sea-Fever"
Christopher Marlowe, "The Passionate Shepherd to His Love"
William Shakespeare, "Sonnet 18"
W. H. Auden, "O What Is That Sound?"
Robert Frost, "Birches"
Walt Whitman, "There Was a Child Went Forth"
Elinor Wylie, "Velvet Shoes"
Algernon C. Swinburne, "A Ballad of Dreamland"
Karl Shapiro, "Drug Store"
Lew Sarrett, "Four Little Foxes"
Edna St. Vincent Millay, "Renascence"
Siegfried Sassoon, "Does It Matter?"
Amy Lowell, "Lilacs"
Langston Hughes, "Jazz Fantasia"
Robert Browning, "Porphyria's Lover"
Francis Thompson, "The Hound of Heaven"
William Wordsworth, "I Wandered Lonely as a Cloud"

Drama

Euripides, *The Trojan Women*. Hecuba's speech beginning "Let lie—the love we seek not is no love . . ."
Euripides, *Iphigenia in Aulis*. Iphigenia's speech beginning "Had I the voice of Orpheus, O my father . . ."
Sophocles, *Antigone*. Creon's speech beginning "Yet would I have thee know that o'er-stubborn spirits . . ." and Antigone's speech beginning "Tomb, bridal-chamber, eternal prison . . ."
Sophocles, *Oedipus*. Oedipus's speech beginning "Thou prayest: and in answer to thy prayer . . ."
Shakespeare, *Hamlet*. Hamlet's speech beginning "Now I am alone . . . ." Act II, Scene 2.
Shakespeare, *Macbeth*. Lady Macbeth's speech begin-

ning "Was the hope drunk wherein you dressed yourself . . ." Act I, Scene 7. Macbeth's speech beginning "Tomorrow and tomorrow . . ." Act V, Scene 5.

Shakespeare, *Antony and Cleopatra*. Cleopatra's speech beginning "Give me my robe . . ." Act V, Scene 2.

Shakespeare, *The Merchant of Venice*. Shylock's speech beginning "Hath not a Jew eyes . . ." Act III, Scene 1, Portia's speech beginning "The quality of mercy is not strained. . . ." Act IV, Scene 1. Lorenzo's speech beginning "How sweet the moonlight on this bank . . ." Act V, Scene 1.

Shakespeare, *The Taming of the Shrew*. Gremio's speech beginning "Tut, she's a lamb, a dove, a fool to him. . . ." Act III, Scene 2.

Shakespeare, *The Tempest*. Prospero's speech beginning "Our revels now are ended . . ." Act IV, Scene 1.

Molière, *Tartuffe*. Dorine's speech beginning "A fine example and a most chaste wife . . ." Act I, Scene 1. Tartuffe's speech beginning "Though I am pious, I am still a man. . . ." Act III, Scene 3.

G. B. Shaw, *Candida*. Candida's speech beginning "Let us sit and talk comfortably over it like three friends." Act III.

G. B. Shaw, *Saint Joan*. Joan's speech beginning "Yes, they told me you were fools . . ." Scene 6.

G. B. Shaw, *Pygmalion*. Doolittle's speech beginning "What am I, Governor's both? . . ." Act II. Liza's speech beginning "I want a little kindness . . ." Act V.

G. B. Shaw, *Back to Methuselah*. Cain's speech beginning "Whose fault was it that I killed Abel? . . ." Act I.

Jerome Kilty, *Dear Liar*. Shaw's speech beginning "22nd February, 1913. What a day! . . ." Act I.

Arthur Miller, *After the Fall*. Quentin's speech at the beginning of the play.

Arthur Miller, *Death of a Salesman*. Linda's speech beginning "I don't say he's a great man. Willy Loman never made a lot of money . . ." Act I, and her final speech at the end of the play.

Tennessee Williams, *The Glass Menagerie*. Tom's speech at the beginning of the play, and Amanda's speech beginning "As you know, I was supposed to be inducted into my office at the D.A.R. . . ." Scene 2, also her telephone conversation in Scene 3.

Eugene O'Neill, *Long Day's Journey into Night*. Several choices.

Anton Chekhov, *The Cherry Orchard*. Madame Ranevskaya's speech beginning "Oh, my sins! I've always thrown my money away . . ." Act II. Trofimov's speech to Anya beginning "All Russia is our garden . . ." Act II, and Lopakhin's speech beginning "I have bought it! . . ." Act III.

Anton Chekhov, *The Three Sisters*. Tchebutykin's speech beginning "The devil take them all—damn them all. They think I am a doctor . . ." Act III.

Anton Chekhov, *Uncle Vanya*. Astrov's speech beginning "I have my own table here, in this house. . . ." Act I.

Oscar Wilde, *The Importance of Being Earnest*. Gwendoline's speech beginning "Ernest, we may never be married! . . ." Act I.

T. S. Eliot, *Murder in the Cathedral*. The speeches of the knights to the audience in Part 2.

Index

Abernathy, R., 20
Aeschylus, 17, 139
Agape, 109
Ajax, 17
Aldrin, E., 20
Anouilh, J., 156
Antigone, 17, 136, 156
Apology, 25
Aristophanes, 26, 107, 134, 136
Armstrong, N., 20
Arnold, M., 148
Articulation, 48–57

Bach, J., 160
Bacon, Francis, 29
Basic gestures, 85, 86
"Before the Beginning of Years," 148, 149
Birds, The, 133, 134
Blake, W., 142
Boleslavsky, R., 31–37
Borge, V., 20
Bourdillon, F., 144
Breathing, 40–43
Brontë, E., 143
Browning, R., 147
Buchwald, A., 20
Bunche, R., 20

Capp, A., 20

Carroll, L., 146
"Chill of the Eve," 144, 145
Choric drama, 114, 117, 120–23
Collins, M., 20
Communication, 62, 63
Concentration, 32–37
Confucius, 27, 105–7

Delsarte, F., 85
Dialect, 48
Dialogues of Plato, 25
Dickinson, E., 145
Diction, 46
Douglas, W., 20
"Dover Beach," 147, 148
Downs, H., 20

Edison, T., 160
Electra, 17, 140, 141
Eliot, T., 120
Espy, R., 20
Euripides, 17
Everyman, 126–30

Frogs, The, 107
Frost, R., 160

Gilbert, W., 131
Glenn, J., 20

173

Goldberg, A., 20
Gregory, D., 20

Hamlet, 48, 80
Hana, 76
Hayakawa, S., 20
Holbrook, H., 20, 162
Hoover, J., 20
House of Usher, 163
Huckleberry Finn, 162
Humphrey, H., 20

Inflection, 70
Intensity, 74
Iolanthe, 131

"Jabberwocky," 146
Jefferson, T., 107, 108
Johnson, A., 125, 127, 139
Johnston College, 15

Kennedy, E., 20
Koran, The, 27

Lao-tse, 28, 105
"Last Lines," 142, 143
"Long, Too Long America," 131
Lysistrata, 134–36

Mark Twain Tonight, 162
Matthew V, 25
Matthew VI, 25
Matthew VII, 25
McCoy, P., 15
Melody, 69, 70
Moscow Arts Theatre, 31
Murder in the Cathedral, 120

Nader, R., 20
"Night Has a Thousand Eyes, The," 144
Nixon, R., 20
Nuance, 76

Oedipus Tyrannus, 17
Of the Training of Children, 24
On the Tranquillity of the Mind, 24

Paine, T., 108
Pause, 68, 69
Peale, N., 20
Pearson, D., 20
Phaedo, 25
"Pied Piper of Hamelin, The," 147
Pitch, 71
Plato, 25, 26
Plutarch, 24
Poe, E., 163
Politics, 106
Presence, 61, 62
Projection, 58–61
Prometheus Bound, 137–39
Pronunciation, 47, 48

Quality, 75

Raitt, J., 20
Rate, 72
Readers' Theatre, 117, 150–54
Relaxation, 38–40
Republic, The, 26
Romeo and Juliet, 92, 93
Rossetti, C., 144
Rubato, 68, 72

Sahl, M., 20
Schirra, W., 20
Seaborg, G., 20
Shakespeare, W., 48
Shaw, G., 160
Socrates, 25
Sophocles, 17, 136, 141
Stage Fright, 61, 62
Stanislavski, C., 74, 91
Stephens, J., 145
Stokowski, L., 160
Stress, 65–67
Swinburne, A., 149

Tempo, 71, 72
Thomas, D., 115, 162
Thomas, L., 20
"Tiger, Tiger," 141, 142
Timing, 87, 88
Tom Sawyer, 162

Toscanini, A., 160

Under Milk Wood, 162
University of Redlands, 15
"Uphill," 143, 144

Verse choir, 117, 120–49
Visual dynamics, 81–84
Voice control, 37
Voice placement, 44–46
Voice production, 43, 44
Voltaire, 28, 29

Volume, 72, 73

Wasps, The, 26
Whitman, W., 131–33
"Word, A," 145
World Without End, 120, 124, 125

Years of the Modern, 131–33
Yugen, 74, 75

Zeami, M., 74, 76